HOW TO VALUE YOUR RESTAURANT

By

Irving L. Blackman, C.P.A., J.D.

Copyright 1989

ISBN 0-929663-01-2

Irving L. Blackman and
The National Restaurant Association
1200 Seventeenth Street, N.W.
Washington, DC 20036

YES...YOU CAN WIN THE VALUATION GAME

When you sell a restaurant in real life, two people — a real seller and a real buyer — negotiate and hammer out a real price. If the two parties can't agree, the seller will simply walk away and look for another buyer.

When you try to value that same business — the one you would have sold in the real world — for tax purposes, the entire perspective changes. It's almost like walking behind the mirror in *Alice in Wonderland.* Indeed, things do get "curiouser and curiouser." Now we must deal with how to evaluate a real restaurant that is to be sold by an imaginary seller (who may be alive or dead, and if dead, represented by his or her heirs or an executor) who will sell to an imaginary buyer....And guess what our simple mission is? All we have to do is come up with a "real" price to be used for tax purposes — a price that was determined in an imaginary deal that was made by imaginary people.

Crazy·as it sounds, that's the way it is. Every business owner, whether he likes it or not, must some day face up to the fact that he will have to value his business for sale or for tax purposes. It can be done voluntarily during life, or it will be done in an involuntary situation, after death, by the IRS. The only "out" is to sell your business in a real transaction during your life. For most restaurant owners, selling doesn't make sense for many reasons. The most common reason is that the typical owner wants to transfer his business to the next generation.

If you want to win the restaurant valuation tax game, this book is for you....keep reading...you (or your family) will save BIG DOLLARS.

Or, maybe you want to sell your business...or buy another business. How do you determine the price to ask or pay? Keep reading.

And finally, as I tell every restaurant owner who comes to my firm for consultation or advice,"If you have any questions, call me."

Untaxingly yours,

Irving L. Blackman, C.P.A., J.D.

Blackman Kallick Bartelstein
300 South Riverside Plaza
Chicago, Illinois 60606
(312) 207-1040

In the following chapters, we have attempted to provide helpful information on a wide range of considerations that are important in buying, selling or transferring a restaurant. It is important to note, however, that the information contained herein is in no way a substitute for the advice and counsel of your attorney and tax adviser. We strongly encourage you to consult with your own attorney and tax adviser prior to making any decision to buy, sell or transfer a restaurant.

For assistance in locating an appraiser, please contact your local CPA Society or the American Society of Appraisers, P.O. Box 17265, Washington, DC 20041, (703) 478-2228. When interviewing business appraisers, be sure that they have the appropriate restaurant appraisal experience because this can differ substantially from general business appraisal.

TABLE OF CONTENTS

CHAPTER I - The Basics of Valuation..1

CHAPTER II - Why Valuations Are a Must...9
Why value your restaurant business for tax purposes?............................11
    Estate taxes...11
    Gifts of closely held stock to family members...............................12
    Buy-sell stock agreements..12
    Sale, purchase or merger...13
    Redemption...13
    Employee stock ownership plans (ESOPs).....................................14
    Divorce property settlement...15
    Other reasons for valuation 15

CHAPTER III - The Legal Approach to Valuation 17

CHAPTER IV - Valuation Methods..29

CHAPTER V - Blending in Your Facts...39

CHAPTER VI - Must Considerations When Valuing Your Restaurant..........47

CHAPTER VII - How to Discount Your Valuation to Save Taxes...................53

CHAPTER VIII - Other Things You Should Know 61
    Legal restrictions on sale of stock...63
    Important hint...63
    Going concern value/goodwill..64
    A word about the IRS and possible penalties.................................65
    How to test your valuation result..66
    Other factors that can affect price (valuation)...............................67

CHAPTER IX - Sample Valuation...69

CHAPTER I

THE BASICS OF VALUATION

If there is an area in the field of taxation where lack of certainty is the hallmark, it is the area of valuation of an interest in a closely held business.

HOW ESTATE TAX CAN DESTROY A FAMILY BUSINESS

Is your restaurant — or are you — worth more than $600,000? Is the business still growing in value? This book is must reading for every restaurant owner who might own all or a portion of his business when he goes to meet his Maker. Why? Because the IRS is your partner when you die. For how much? That depends on how much you will be worth.

The first $600,000 of an estate escapes tax. Then your partner — the IRS — starts to get its share.

Let's run through an example. After you finish reading the example, you should get a ballpark estimate on your own potential estate tax liability.

EXAMPLE
Today your business is worth $500,000. Some day, when you go to that big restaurant in the sky, your earthly business may be worth more. All things being equal, inflation and growth are likely to ratchet the value of your business into seven figures. How much will the tax be? Assume you have other property worth $600,000 on the day you die and that your wife went to her reward before you did. The following schedule shows the federal estate tax bite:

If Your Business Is Worth*	The Estate Tax Will Be	Tax Bracket If Excess
$ 500,000	$ 194,000	41%
1,000,000	408,000	45
1,500,000	637,000	49
2,000,000	886,000	53
2,500,000	1,153,000	55

*The value of the total estate is $600,000 more than the amount shown for the worth of the business. In effect, the first $600,000 of your estate is tax free.

Okay, using this schedule, estimate your own estate tax liability. If you are typical, your most valued asset is your business.

Now, at least you have an idea of the potential size of the valuation problem.

The obvious question is — "Where will the money come from to pay the tax?" Unfortunately, the money is often just not there.

Because the potential tax stakes are so high, placing a value on the interest (usually stock) of an owner of a closely held business (usually a corporation) often leads to serious conflict with the Internal Revenue Service. The IRS seldom agrees with the taxpayer's value. Valuation is sort of a game — one without clearly defined rules. The score is kept in dollars — *your dollars.* Unlike publicly traded stock, where the value is published in the daily paper, the value of closely held stock must be individually determined. All too often this can hurt the business owner. Here is the typical result of a business' value determined:

1. By the IRS . . . . Much higher than the value
reported by the taxpayer.
2. By the taxpayer. . . . . Much lower than the value
claimed by the IRS agents.

3. By the courts. . . . . . . Somewhere in between.

The schedule in the example we just looked at gives you an idea of the size of the tax payments that may hinge on the outcome of a dispute with the IRS. Professional fees for the fight are high. Result? Business liquidations (at sacrifice prices) sometimes become necessary to pay estate taxes because a deceased owner failed to foresee the high value the IRS could successfully claim for his closely held stock.

AN OVERVIEW OF VALUATION AND TAXES

Welcome to the world of uncertainty.

Let's identify some of the uncertainties we professionals face in most valuation situations:

1. We are uncertain about when, if ever, the client will sell the business.
2. We are uncertain about how long the client will live.
3. We are uncertain if business will get better or worse.
4. We are uncertain about the rate of inflation.
5. We are uncertain about what estate tax bracket the client will be in when he dies.

The list of uncertainties could go on and on, but you get the idea. Death tends to bring certainty. The moment of truth for valuation purposes will have arrived. All that would remain to be done is to apply the appropriate estate tax bracket to the final valuation.

Every business owner, whether he likes it or not, must some day face up to the fact that he will have to value his business for tax purposes. The only "out" is to sell his business in a real transaction during his life. For most business owners, however, selling doesn't make sense for many reasons. The two most common reasons are: One, the typical business owner wants to transfer his business to the next generation, or two, he wants to keep on working until he dies.

VALUATION IN GENERAL

The valuation of an investment is based upon the investor's calculation and expectation of approximately what return on his investment he will garner over some future time frame. This is true whether it is a commodities futures contract bought in the morning and sold that afternoon, a long-term bond held for decades or an operating business. This principle — future expectation of return on investment — is the foundation of valuation. A buyer determines the value of a commodity — how much he wants to pay for it today — based upon the rate of return he thinks his investment will make for him over a future period of time.

The next few paragraphs and examples are somewhat simplistic. Yet, they are extremely important as a base on which this report builds in later chapters.

The rate of return on an investment is the percentage earned on the amount of money invested. The higher the percentage, the higher the rate of return. The higher the expected rate of return on an investment in a commodity, the more value it has, and the higher the price the investor is willing to pay for it. The lower the rate of return, the lower the price the investor will pay. For the moment only, assume the investment has no risk.

EXAMPLE

Two 10-year term bonds each have a face value of $1,000. The average rate of interest, or market rate, paid by such bonds is 10%. However, one bond pays 5% interest, while the other pays 15%. An investor would be willing to pay more than $1,000 for the bond yielding 15% and less than $1,000 for the bond yielding 5%. The amount of money over the face value of the 15% bond that the investor would pay is called bond premium. The amount below face value that an investor would pay for the 5% bond is called bond discount. In this case, to equal the 10% market rate, the value of the 15% bond would include a premium ($561.58) and would sell for $1,561.58, while the 5% bond would sell for $691.26 because of a $308.74 discount.

The price of a closely held business is determined in much the same manner. It is the future earning power of a business, as a going concern, that determines its worth to a buyer and sets the price he is willing to pay.

Again, only for the moment, assume no risk and that the earning power of the business is the only factor being considered.

EXAMPLE

Suppose a restaurant has a book value of $1 million and over the past five years has returned 20% on the owner's investment. A buyer would be willing to pay a premium over that book value because he highly values the sustained, proven earning power of the business. Suppose instead, however, that an identical business with the same book value has returned only 2% over a five-year period. A seller would have to be willing to discount the value of the business in order to lure the cash for the sale out of a willing buyer's pocket.

The purpose of this book is to illustrate how a buyer or a seller, a taxpayer or the IRS, or a borrower or a lender arrives at the right premium or discount when valuing a business. If you can keep the basic principle of valuation firmly in mind — future expectation of return on investment — the process becomes one of fine-tuning the price of the business using as many factors as necessary to fit the specific purpose of the valuation.

Anyone considering a valuation should also heed these two cliches: "One man's sorrow is another man's gain," and "Nothing is etched in stone." Why?

1. Any valuation usually has two adversaries valuing a business for diametrically opposite purposes. A particular fact that one party puts great stock in may be horse feathers to the other party.

2. Valuations are determined at a certain point in time and wedded to a specific purpose. The passage of time usually makes any valuation as useless as yesterday's papers.

It is the combination of these two factors that makes valuation more of an art than a science.

THE CLOSELY HELD BUSINESS IN GENERAL

In essence, the principle that underlies the valuation of a closely held business is the same principle that underlies the valuation of any investment. *Businesses are valuable not because of what they have done, but because of what they are capable of doing.* It is the future expectation of the rate of return that a business can generate that determines its value.

If there is an area in the field of taxation where lack of certainty is the hallmark, it is the area of valuation of an interest in a closely held business. This causes frustration to accountants, who are used to adding and subtracting precise numbers and coming up with results that produce sheets that are in balance. This also frustrates lawyers, who are used to finding cases in point that, when taken in series, produce a brief that neatly proves their clients' case. Probably the most frustrated of all is the poor tax-payer/client — uncertainty reigns supreme, and often the financial life of a business and a family hangs in the balance.

Every company to be valued has its own set of facts and circumstances, and each valuation is unique and different from every other valuation. Two companies in the same business with almost identical numbers can have significantly different values because of just one fact difference. No set of general rules or volumes of books can bring out the importance of unique facts.

The valuation process is an art, not a science, but just as art has its discipline, so too does valuation. The discipline lies mainly in approaches and techniques rather than some magic formula or an all-too-easy reference to market prices of so-called comparable businesses. Our inquiry will not only be on how to select the right approach, but on how to attain the desired results for the business owner or his family.

THE RESTAURANT BUSINESS

Everything we have said about a closely held business, in general, applies to the valuation of a restaurant. As a result, the valuation of your business must be taken seriously by each of you. Someday you will be called, without warning, to your ultimate place up above. Your estate must be planned before the call. For most readers, your business will be the biggest asset in your estate. If the IRS wins a valuation battle, your family loses. Everything you worked a lifetime to build could be dismantled overnight just to pay taxes.

Ingredients for a Successful Valuation

The valuation of a restaurant and the tax impact of such a valuation are like oil and water — not very good for mixing. Your mission— should you choose to accept it — is to learn how to make the mix work.

Two ingredients are essential for a successful valuation tax mission:
1. Knowledge and
2. The right professional.

> *IMPORTANT*
> This subject — valuation — is not a game for amateurs. For your best interest, and that of your family, use a competent professional.

This book will give you the knowledge necessary to select the right professional appraiser.

ROLE OF THE APPRAISER

An appraiser is needed whenever a restaurant must be valued, but will not be the subject of an arm's length transaction (between a real seller and a real buyer) on the valuation date. No one will ever know for sure what the business would have sold for (the real fair market value) on the valuation date. Hence an appraisal, at best only an opinion, is the only known way to fix the fair market value in a non-arm's length transaction.

The prime reason for such an undertaking is to approximate the price the business would command if there was an active public market for it (ending in a real sale to a real buyer). Such an endeavor is necessarily complex and often sophisticated since it involves many subjective decisions. The business owner in need of an appraisal is well advised to supplement his own impressions of what he believes his business to be worth with the opinion of an independent professional adviser. YOUR BEST BET — *use an adviser who knows and understands your industry.*

Since it is only an opinion, even though an "expert" one, an appraisal is subject to attack. Assuming a competent appraiser, the appraisal is only as good as the research on which it is based and the rationale employed. Any honest appraiser knows there is a range of values for a given business or asset. He also realizes he is not all-knowing, no matter how carefully he works. The appraiser is an advocate. His job is to come up with the value that serves the ends of his client, within the range of values that is reasonable. No doubt there will be an appraiser on the other side who will, within the range of reason, come up with a value at the other end of the scale.

In performing a valuation, the professional appraiser should critically review all information available, including the business' financial statements, availability of labor, the present and potential market and customer base, industry reports, management interviews and other pertinent data. The valuation should be based on all the relevant facts. The appraiser must use common sense and informed judgment in the valuation methodology to weigh those facts and determine their overall significance.

Opposing viewpoints will be aired, concessions will be made, factors will be examined in light of new understanding generated by the controversy and out of this will come the agreed-upon appraised value. The appraiser who prevails will usually be the one who has best done his homework. The winner will be the business owner and his family.

NECESSITY FOR WRITTEN APPRAISAL

It is essential to go beyond the mere numbers that appear on the balance sheet and operating statement of the business to be valued. The numbers alone rarely tell the full valuation story. The emphasis must always be on a careful analysis of the underlying factors that produce the final valuation.

Selection of Appraiser

Many hours of investigation, discussion, research and thinking are required to form a basis for a valuation. All too often the value figure finally selected for a tax return or other document is the result of ideas produced in emotion-packed brainstorming sessions among accountants, lawyers and key employees of the company rather than a detailed logical analysis that covers all bases. A far better technique is to select an experienced, independent appraiser who knows and understands the industry in which the business operates. Ask your banker, lawyer, accountant or trade association to refer you to an appraiser. Then, give the person selected full responsibility for developing and proving a valuation figure.

Content of Appraisal

Of utmost importance is the manner in which the appraisal is presented. It must, of course, be in writing and should include a statement of the qualifications of the appraiser as well as a statement of the scope of his investigation. If the valuation is for estate or gift tax purposes, it should be submitted with the applicable tax return.

Often, the primary emphasis is on a detailed description of the company. Corporate history should be traced from date of inception to valuation date, including development of products, locations and growth in sales and physical facilities. Differences in operating results from year to year should be analyzed both from the standpoint of the company and the economy. To make it easier for the reader to grasp trends, the appraisal should contain — at an appropriate point in the text — a summary of sales and operating results for at least the most recent five-year period.

Often, the mere description of the company, its products, sales and assets will comprise most of the content of the appraisal. This is just as essential as the analysis of the numbers comprising the earnings and the assets. In the end the valuation is based on logical conclusions supported by both numbers and the underlying facts.

The appraiser should reveal in the appraisal every fact that has a bearing on valuation. If an IRS agent makes an independent investigation and comes up with facts that significantly alter the valuation, the credibility of the appraiser and the appraisal is gone. The appraisal will convince the agent only if he senses that the full story has been told. If it has, the agent's independent investigation will confirm and solidify the appraiser's valuation.

There are at least two distinct advantages to a complete written appraisal:

1. The taxpayer's representatives will have all their thinking contained in one complete document. The IRS audit will not occur until many months after the return is filed, when memories of conversations and vaguely developed theories will be dim. It is far better to have the complete position of the taxpayer developed initially and recorded for later use.

2. To the extent that the appraisal is factually complete, it will save the IRS agent the trouble of demanding information from the taxpayer and will give the taxpayer better credibility.

That's it — the basic approach to the valuation of closely held businesses.

CHAPTER II

WHY VALUATIONS ARE A MUST

What your business is worth is a critical question at many turns in your business and personal life; the question even survives your death.

WHY VALUE YOUR RESTAURANT BUSINESS FOR TAX PURPOSES?

So you want to value your business. First, you must answer a question. What is the purpose of the valuation? Are you a buyer?...seller?...or is the valuation for tax purposes? If you are a buyer or seller, your estimation of value will be naturally prejudiced. A similar prejudice is present for tax purposes. Why?...Because all mistakes are paid to an imaginary buyer — the IRS.

When and for Whom?

Bear in mind that a valuation is always:

1. As of a particular point in time —
A difference of only a few months in the valuation date can introduce (or eliminate) a fact of crucial significance.

2. For a particular purpose —
There is no such thing as a valuation that will serve the purpose of everyone who might have an interest in it.

Why Periodic Valuations Are a Must

Without reliable knowledge of the value of his stock, a restaurant owner cannot:

1. Plan effectively to minimize estate taxes.
2. Develop an effective gift program of property to family members.
3. Negotiate proper buy-sell stock agreements.
4. Negotiate realistically for possible sales, purchases or mergers.
5. Use a redemption to transfer ownership to the next generation.
6. Create an ESOP to sell all or part of the business to the employees.
7. Satisfy the court that both spouses received a "fair share" of the business in a divorce action.
8. Implement other required purposes; for example, collateral for a loan or value at date of death for estate tax purposes.

Let's examine some of these points individually to see why they are so important.

A. Estate Taxes

A reasonably sound knowledge of the value of your company's stock is essential for minimizing estate taxes, providing adequate liquidity for both federal and state death taxes and assuring that estate expenses can be met while keeping the corporation economically sound and continuing to produce income for the heirs. Misjudgments usually place a severe financial burden on the business and in extreme cases require liquidation.

HOW TO BEAT THE ESTATE TAX — PLANNING TOOLS

The estate tax is a transfer tax. It is levied on the closely held business owner's property that is transferred to his heirs or others when he dies. Transferring a closely held business at the least tax cost could be the subject of another book altogether, yet it and valuation of the business are inextricably intertwined.

As the years go by, my office has seen and continues to see three types of tax disaster problems that plague restaurant owners in the transfer area:

1. The transfer isn't done because the founder doesn't know how to solve the particular transfer problem, which compounds as the potential tax cost continues to mount.
2. Procrastination.
3. The transfer has been made, but it was wrong from a tax standpoint, and the

owner, business or the family has been or will be clobbered taxwise.

However, never fear. The government-transfer-tax-machine can be beaten.

A variety of tax-saving transfer-of-ownership techniques have been used by so-called "sophisticated business people" for generations. Their use has been limited to those fortunate few who have been able to translate their objectives and applicable tax law into a workable transfer plan. The sooner the plan is put into effect, the greater the tax savings.

In most cases, planning the transfer of a closely held corporation means freezing the owner's estate. A good transfer plan is part of an overall estate plan that attempts to get the asset-freezing process into place as soon as possible. Obviously, if you can cut off wealth before it accumulates, serious tax problems can be avoided.

Asset freezing is really a generic term for describing the various tools that have been designed to limit the estate tax value of a closely held business. The typical freeze has three objectives:

1. Transferring future growth;
2. Providing the owner a flow of income during his life; and
3. Keeping him in control of the business for as long as he lives.

These are both transfer and valuation tools. An asset freeze simply seeks to achieve all or almost all of the owner's specific objectives. The freeze is usually the most important part of a transfer plan. Following is a list of popular transfer tools (items B through E) requiring a valuation.

B. Gifts of Closely Held Stock to Family Members

Knowing the value of a restaurant's business helps the owner decide whether he should establish a program of selective gifts to family members or, perhaps, trusts for the benefit of family members. Whether the restaurant owner wishes to spread income among other family members (who are generally in lower income tax brackets) or to decrease the amount of stock retained in his estate (in order to reduce estate taxes), the fair market value of the business must be ascertained.

The donor (the person making the gift) of closely held stock can transfer stock worth up to $10,000 annually ($20,000 if the donor's spouse consents to the gift) to each donee (the person receiving the gift) without paying gift tax. Such gifts save estate taxes in two ways: (1) The value of the stock will not be subject to the estate tax when the donor dies, and (2) any appreciation in the stock after the gift is made also escapes estate tax.

That portion of an annual gift over $10,000 ($20,000 if married) will be included in the donor's estate.

C. Buy-Sell Stock Agreements

A typical buy-sell agreement is:

1. A contract between shareholders of a closely held corporation (or between the shareholders and the corporation itself), in which the parties agree;
2. That any shareholder transferring corporate stock — because of death, disability, gift, bankruptcy or any other reason — must sell or transfer the shares;
3. To the other shareholders (or the corporation) at a specified price and on specified terms.

If the agreement is structured properly, that price will be honored by the courts as the correct valuation of the deceased's closely held stock for estate tax purposes. The courts have held that for estate tax purposes the IRS is bound to honor the price specified in the buy-sell agreement if the following conditions are met:

1. The price of the shares fixed in the buy-sell agreement has been set according to

some reasonable valuation method.

2. The agreement has a ***bona fide*** business purpose and is not, in the IRS' words, "a device to pass the decedent's shares to the natural objects of his bounty for less than adequate and full consideration"; in other words, the agreement is not a testamentary device used to defeat the estate tax. This issue is raised by the IRS when the parties to the agreement are related (especially parents and children).

3. The estate of the deceased is legally bound to sell the shares to the parties specified in the agreement after the shareholder's death.

4. The parties to the agreement cannot dispose of their stock in their lifetime unless the other parties have a right of first refusal.

If careful drafting does not satisfy the above requirements, the IRS is free to use its own valuation method to arrive at what is usually a higher value for the stock (Reg. 20.2031-2(h); *Estate of O.B. Littick*, 31 TC 181, 1958).

D. Sale, Purchase or Merger

1. Sale or Purchase

The sale or purchase of a restaurant calls for the application of the appraisal techniques described in detail in this book as well as the utilization of a competent, professional appraiser. Those techniques are the heart and soul of this book.

2. Merger

Most states allow corporations to merge. A not uncommon scenario involves the merger of a closely held corporation into a publicly held corporation or the merger of two closely held corporations. The shareholders of the former corporation usually exchange their shares for shares of the surviving corporation. Valuation of these shares is important for tax purposes and for protecting and satisfying minority shareholder rights.

State law usually provides that shareholders of the corporation who would cease to exist after the merger have a right to a court hearing to determine whether the price offered for the stock by the surviving corporation is adequate. That hearing usually turns into a battle of valuation experts, not unlike psychiatrists testifying as to the sanity of a defendant in a criminal trial. The difference is that the value of the closely held corporation's stock, not a defendant's state of mind, is the bone of contention.

E. Redemption

A redemption occurs when a shareholder sells some or all of his stock back to the corporation. The corporation is said to "redeem" (buy) the stock. The proceeds from the sale are treated as dividends to the shareholder unless:

1. The number of shares redeemed is disproportionate to the number of shares held by the shareholder;

2 The redemption terminates the shareholder's entire interest in the corporation;

3. The redemption is not substantially equivalent to a dividend; or

4. The redemption is made to a non-corporate shareholder in partial liquidation.

If the redemption falls into any of the four categories, it is treated as a sale or exchange. Result: Any property or cash received by the shareholder that results in a profit is taxed as a capital gain.

A REDEMPTION SCENARIO

Joe Owner's son owns a small number of shares, which he purchased from Joe or received as a gift. Joe sells (redeems) the balance of his shares to the corporation. The selling (redemption) of all of Joe's shares qualifies under the second exemption above — it is a complete termination of his interest in the corporation.

This method accomplishes the freeze — son owns 100 percent of the future growth. However, there are some drawbacks: Joe realizes a capital gain on the profit, and the corporation cannot deduct the payments. Not only is Joe out of control, but the tax rules prohibit him from working for the corporation for 10 years. What if he does? The capital gain may turn into ordinary income — a tax disaster under the rules prior to the Tax Reform Act of 1986. I still think there is a strong possibility that the benefits of capital gains will be retained by another change in the tax law.

EXAMPLE

A husband and wife who were the sole shareholders in a family corporation had all their stock in the company redeemed and, at the same time, resigned all of their positions as directors and officers of the company. Their son became the sole shareholder. Unfortunately, at the request of the son, the father continued to work for the company as a salaried adviser at a $1,000-a-month salary.

That continued advisory capacity was enough to constitute an "interest in the corporation" that turned the father's capital gain into ordinary income.

What this case illustrates is that redemptions, an effective tool for freezing the owner's interest in a corporation if done properly, carry with them severe disadvantages for the closely held business owner who desires to continue working in his business or who wants to nurture the next generation into the reins of ownership (*L.V. Seda*, 82 TC 484).

F. Employee Stock Ownership Plans (ESOPs)

If the owner, for whatever reason, does not want to, or cannot transfer his corporation to his family, an ESOP might be the answer. ESOPs can be used to facilitate the transfer of a closely held corporation to non-family buyers or the company's employees by creating a market for its shares. Best of all, the owner can take cash out of the corporation as a capital gain or defer the gain by reinvesting the ESOP distribution in domestic common stocks.

An ESOP is a qualified defined contribution plan, which is similar to a typical profit-sharing plan, but it is designed to invest primarily in the employer's stock or securities. Technically, an ESOP can be either a stock bonus plan or a combination stock bonus and money purchase pension plan.

Here's an overview of a common method of operating an ESOP:

1. An employee stock ownership trust (ESOT) is established by the employer.
2. The ESOT invests in (purchases) the employer's stock or securities. The ESOT can acquire the employer's stock from:
    a. The stockholders of the employer corporation;
    b. The employer corporation; or
    c. Both.
3. The ESOT can get the cash for the purchase either:
    a. By a direct deductible contribution to the ESOT from the employer or
    b. By borrowing the money from a bank.
4. Subsequent contributions to the ESOT, which are used to pay off principal and interest on funds borrowed to purchase employer stock, are deductible by the employer corporation as made.

The ESOT, with all the rights and benefits of a shareholder, holds the stock for the benefit of participating employees. The stock is distributed to the participants when they are eligible to receive it, upon retirement, disability or death. Usually, the ESOT or the corporation repurchases the distributed stock from the employees. This flow of stock "to, from and back" to the trust or corporation, combined with very favorable tax breaks, makes the ESOP an interesting planning tool.

The Tax Reform Act of 1984 and the Tax Reform Act of 1986 give ESOPs a number of new tax breaks. You now have a way to help defeat the estate tax; an ESOP can acquire employer securities from a deceased shareholder in return for the assumption of his estate tax liability (Code Sec. 2210). This liability can be deferred over 15 years in some instances. In addition, 50 percent of the value of stock sold to an ESOT after death can be excluded from your estate. There are other goodies in these laws for ESOPs. See your professional adviser. Valuation of the employer securities sold to the ESOP is crucial to determination of the estate tax liability.

G. Divorce Property Settlement

Divorce, in and of itself, can be an unpleasant experience. If one or both of the divorcing spouses own a closely held business, reaching a property settlement can cause a financial explosion.

Suppose, for example, that one spouse knows that the other has depreciated the business' assets heavily at an accelerated rate or has depressed income by use of excessive entertainment expense deductions. That spouse will be reluctant, and rightly so, to accept any valuation that does not make appropriate adjustments for these factors.

The property settlement usually ends up with one spouse transferring stock in the corporation to the other. Valuation of the stock is the cornerstone to reaching a settlement. The parties relying upon the valuation are in conflict, often accompanied by bitterness. This only makes the valuation more difficult.

What are the tax consequences of transferring stock of a closely held corporation as a property settlement? Here are the rules: No gain or loss is recognized to either spouse on the transfer of property between them incident to divorce. The receiving spouse takes a carryover basis in the transferred property.

EXAMPLE

Joe owns 100% of the stock of Go-Go Co. Joe's tax basis is $200,000, but Go-Go is now worth $2,200,000. Joe transfers 25% of Go-Go, with a value of $550,000, to Mary — his wife — as a part of a property settlement.

These are the immediate happy tax consequences: Joe recognizes no gain or loss. He can use appreciated property, Go-Go, at its fair market value to fulfill his divorce obligations with no adverse tax consequences. However, Mary steps into Joe's shoes as owner of the transferred stock and is stuck with his low basis. If Mary sells the stock for its present value, she will suffer a taxable capital gain of $500,000 ($550,000 value less $50,000 tax basis).

Frequently, the net result is that the dispute over the valuation ends up in court, with both parties spending money on attorneys' and accountants' fees that they should be dividing between themselves instead. Periodic valuations made before the divorce can narrow the range of disputed value between the parties and make a settlement easier to reach.

H. Other Reasons for Valuation

1. Charitable Gifts

Contributions of appreciated stock to charity can be very attractive taxwise to the business owner. He must plan such gifts properly so that they (a) do not deplete his cash reserves and (b) at the same time give him a cash benefit through reduction of his federal income tax. Among the planning considerations are: (a) the loss of some percentage of voting control weighed against the income tax advantages, (b) the lifetime cash flow advantage to the owner and (c) his estate tax benefit realized by removing the stock from his estate. Not surprisingly, the IRS takes a keen interest in the valuation of such contributed shares.

2. Reorganization of a Troubled Business

Often, a restaurant finds itself cash poor and unable to meet current obligations, yet projects a profitable future. A restructuring of its capital may make it more attractive for financing short-term as well as long-term obligations to reassure creditors that the business will pay its liabilities.

3. Obtaining Financing

A lender is more apt to furnish capital funds to a business if that business can demonstrate that it possesses valuable assets, whether operating or intangible, and that it also generates substantial revenue and profit from those assets. Valuations that show these factors over and above what is shown on the business' financial statements can make obtaining financing easier.

4. Buy-Out of Dissident Minority Shareholders

Most states have laws that protect the interests of minority shareholders. Often, articles of incorporation provide for contingent buy-outs of minority interests. Valuations of such minority interests that fairly reflect value minimize costly court battles that impose a financial drain on the operations of the business and often cast a cloud of uncertainty over the business' future.

Valuation of minority interests usually must be discounted for lack of marketability. See Chapter VII.

5. Spin-Off of the Closely Held Business

Sometimes it becomes necessary to spin off (sell) a division or subsidiary of a business for a number of reasons, such as:

   a. Compliance with government agency regulations (SEC, IRS, FTC, etc.);
   b. Infusion of working capital into the parents' closely held business; and
   c. Resolution of disputes between shareholders regarding the operations and objectives of the business.

The transaction can be tax-free if it is for a legitimate business purpose. Whether tax-free or not, valuation is necessary to justify the selling price, number of shares to be received and the value of the business as a whole and the portion being spun off.

And Finally—

Yes, there are many more reasons as to why a business should be or must be valued. Whatever the valuation reason may be, the relationship of the parties, the objectives to be accomplished and a host of other factors that vary with the circumstances will cause the fair market value to fluctuate, depending on the eyes of the beholder. Honest, competent people can and do come up with different ideas for fair market value. The IRS will take various postures leading to a high or low value, depending on the possible generation of more tax revenue. On the other hand, taxpayers, aided and abetted by their professionals, will similarly seek a value that best serves their ends.

What then is the purpose of the valuation? Quite simply, it is to serve the ends of the client/taxpayer....for us, that means you — the owner of a restaurant.

CHAPTER III

THE LEGAL APPROACH TO VALUATION

These are the rules according to the IRS and the courts. Nothing is definite. At best, you have only guideposts.

VALUATION AS THE IRS SEES IT

In every valuation of a restaurant for tax purposes, it is Uncle Sam (in the form of the IRS) who will look over your shoulder. The way to win the valuation game is to know in advance what the IRS wants to see.

There are three sources the IRS looks to: (1) the Internal Revenue Code, (2) Regulations and (3) Rulings. Overseeing both the IRS and taxpayers are the courts. Actually, including the courts, there are four sources that make up the body of valuation law. This chapter and the balance of the book will often look to one or more of these sources as the authority for a particular position. Telling you where your professional can find the authority is called a "cite." These cites appear throughout this book.

THE CLOSELY HELD CORPORATION — DEFINITION

This book concerns itself with the closely held business. Although a closely held business can be any one of many entities (such as a partnership, sole proprietorship, joint venture, etc.), this book focuses its attention on the closely held corporation. The same valuation principles that apply to *closely held corporations* apply to unincorporated closely held businesses such as sole proprietorships, partnerships or joint ventures. An IRS valuation ruling (Rev. Rul. 65-192) specifically states that the same principles are applicable to all closely held businesses of whatever legal form.

The closely held corporation has been defined by the IRS as:
"A corporation whose market quotations are either unavailable or of such scarcity that they do not reflect the fair market value" (Rev. Rul. 59-60).

"A corporation...the shares of which are owned by a relatively limited number of stockholders. Often the entire stock issue is held by one family. The result of this situation is that little, if any, trading in the shares takes place. There is, therefore, no established market for the stock, and such sales as occur at irregular intervals seldom reflect all the elements of a representative transaction as defined by the term *fair market value*" (Rev. Rul. 59-60).

THE MEANING OF "FAIR MARKET VALUE"

In every valuation matter before the IRS, you must be concerned with the meaning of "fair market value." For purposes of the estate tax (Reg. 20.2031-1(b)) and gift tax (Reg. 25.2512-1), fair market value is defined as:
"The price at which the property would change hands between a willing buyer and a willing seller when the former is not under any compulsion to buy and the latter is not under any compulsion to sell, both parties having reasonable knowledge of relevant facts."

As a practical matter, it is impossible to pinpoint the exact price two parties would arrive at in an actual transaction. This is particularly true when a major block of stock is involved because the price agreed upon is normally determined through a bargaining process. In addition to the underlying economics of the company and its industry, the bargaining skill and the individual circumstances of the two parties would also affect the actual price. These highly subjective considerations make a valuation study by an independent analyst imprecise, at best.

The key question is:
Who has the advantage when the uncontested fact is that "fair market value" is

a matter of uncertainty, floating on a wavy sea of opinion?...the IRS?...the tax-payer?...the owner of a restaurant? I maintain the advantage is clearly on your side — the taxpayer/business owner — but you must know what you are doing.

Many sections of the Internal Revenue Code refer to fair market value, but neither these sections nor the applicable regulations give any precise definition. Most practitioners assume that the definition for estate and gift tax purposes is universally applicable, and so far this assumption has proved correct.

Way back in 1928, the court (in *James Couzens,* 11 BTA 1040) really said it like it is:
"It has been said that value is a price at which a willing seller and a willing buyer would agree to trade if they both were aware of the facts....Recognizing all the facts in existence, and from them attempting reasonably to predict those to come, being neither unduly skeptical nor unduly optimistic, we sought to determine what an intelligent and reasonable seller and an intelligent and reasonable buyer would in their fairly mercenary interests have been most likely to agree upon as a price for the property in question."

In the real world, when valuing the stocks of closely held corporations for federal tax purposes, instead of a mythical willing seller and a mythical willing buyer, we have as traditional adversaries real taxpayers (or their heirs or donees) and the "real" IRS. The many litigated cases and the more numerous compromise settlements clearly show each adversary considers the other anything but willing and reasonable.

Estate Tax Code Section

Section 2031(b) of the Code, covering valuation for estate purposes of unlisted securities, provides:
"In the case of stock and securities of a corporation the value of which, by reason of their not being listed on an exchange and by reason of the absence of sales thereof, cannot be determined with reference to bid and asked prices or with reference to sales prices, the value thereof shall be determined by taking into consideration, in addition to all other factors, the value of stock or securities of corporations engaged in the same or a similar line of business which are listed on an exchange."

Estate Tax Regulations

The estate tax regulations (Reg. 20.2031.2-(f)) provide:
"Where selling prices or bid and asked prices are unavailable. If the provisions of paragraphs (b), (c), and (d) of this section are inapplicable because actual sale prices and bona fide bid and asked prices are lacking, then the fair market value is to be determined by taking the following factors into consideration:

1. In the case of corporation or other bonds, the soundness of the security, the interest yield, the date of maturity, and other relevant factors; and
2. In the case of shares of stock, the company's net worth, prospective earning power and dividend-paying capacity, and other relevant factors.

"Some of the 'other relevant factors' referred to in subparagraphs (1) and (2) of this paragraph are: the goodwill of the business; the economic outlook in the particular industry and its management; the degree of control of the business represented by the block of stock to be valued; and the values of securities of corporations engaged in the same or similar lines of business which are listed on a stock exchange. However, the weight to be accorded such comparisons or any other evidentiary factors considered in the determination of a value depends upon the facts of each case. Complete financial and other data upon which the valuation is based should be submitted with the return, including copies of reports of any examinations of the company made by accountants, engineers, or any technical experts as of or near the applicable valuation date."

These regulations (Reg. 20.2031-3) further provide:

"Valuation of interests in business. The fair market value of any interest of a decedent in a business, whether a partnership or a proprietorship, is a net amount which a willing purchaser, whether an individual or a corporation, would pay for the interest to a willing seller, neither being under any compulsion to buy or to sell and both having reasonable knowledge of relevant facts. The net value is determined on the basis of all relevant factors including:

a. A fair appraisal as of the applicable valuation date of all the assets of the business, tangible and intangible, including goodwill;
b. The demonstrated earning capacity of the business; and
c. The other factors set forth in paragraphs (f) and (h) of Reg. 20.2031.2 relating to the valuation of corporate stock, to the extent applicable."

Gift Tax Regulations
The gift tax regulations (25.2512.2(f) and 25.2512.3) dealing with the valuation of stocks of closely held corporations and business interests in partnerships and sole proprietorships are similar to those for estate tax valuations.

IRS Ruling on Valuations
The Internal Revenue Service rulings for determining the valuation of closely held businesses contain the most important guidelines that must be considered. The important rulings are analyzed in depth in this book.

The Early IRS Rulings
The first federal income tax law pushed its way into the American way of life on March 1, 1913. By 1920 the first business valuation regulation made its appearance.

Rigid Formula Approach
The IRS first tried to set valuation criteria by issuing Appeals and Review Memoranda (ARM) 34 in 1920. The theory of ARM 34 was that a business is expected to earn a normal profit on its tangible assets and that any actual profit greater than normal profit must be attributed to intangible assets. ARM 34 thus distinguished between tangible and intangible assets and attributed a set value to each.

This was done by use of a rigid formula. To the IRS, normal profit on the net book value of tangible assets was between 8 percent and 10 percent, and the proper profit on intangibles was between 15 percent and 20 percent.

EXAMPLE
If a business with $200,000 in tangible assets earned $25,000 a year and its normal profit (according to the IRS) should have been $16,000 (8% of $200,000), then $9,000 ($25,000 – $16,000) was its profit on intangible assets. If the $9,000 profit on intangible assets was capitalized at 15% (100% ÷ 15% = 6-2/3), this produced $60,000 (6-2/3 x $9,000), the value of the intangible assets. The $60,000 in intangible assets was then added to the $200,000 in tangible assets to produce a value of $260,000 for the business.

It should be obvious that the only thing to recommend the use of ARM 34 was its disarming simplicity. The appraiser did not have to know anything about the business, its plant, inventory, customers, product lines, quality of management or competition or anything about the state of the economy. All he had to know was how to multiply and divide. A high school student could, in a matter of minutes, compute with precision the value of a company with $10 million in sales.

ARM 34 was the outcome of a quest for precision rather than a search for the truth. ARM 34 makes no sense when tangible assets have a true value that is different (higher or lower) from that carried on the books, and this is true for at least some assets of every corporation. It does not distinguish between capital-intensive and labor-intensive businesses. It arbitrarily assigns practically the same rate of return to all businesses, when one economic fact of life is that real businesses earn far different rates of return depending on a whole host of factors.

For these and many other reasons, ARM 34 was strongly contested by practitioners and was never accorded great weight by the courts. Gradually, the IRS relaxed its insistence on the use of ARM 34 and finally (Rev. Rul. 65-192) formally limited its use.

Later Rulings

The next important ruling affecting the valuation of closely held corporations was Rev. Rul. 54-77 issued in 1954. This ruling discussed many factors to be considered in the determination of "fair market value," based on experiences of the Internal Revenue Service and numerous court cases. The ruling was superseded in 1959 by Rev. Rul. 59-60. This 1959 ruling is currently the most important single source of IRS dogma dealing with the valuation of a closely held business.

The Most Important IRS Ruling

This is where the valuation action is. Recognizing that simplistic formulas are invalid, the IRS issued Rev. Rul. 59-60, which is now the most significant legal guideline in valuations. At least, it is the place to start in determining the value of a business.

Judgmental Use of Many Economic Factors

Just a few pages ago you read that Section 2031(b) tells us that to value a closely held corporation requires consideration of the value of stock or securities of corporations, engaged in the same or similar line of business, that are listed on an exchange in addition to all other factors. To consider "all other factors" is an endless task. One of the principal aids in determining what "other factors" means is Rev. Rul. 59-60.

This ruling lists eight factors to consider in valuing a closely held business:
1. The nature of the business and the history of the enterprise from its inception;
2. The economic outlook in general and the condition and outlook of the specific industry in particular;
3. The book value of the stock and the financial condition of the business;
4. The earnings capacity of the company;
5. The company's dividend-paying capacity;
6. Whether the enterprise has goodwill or other intangible value;
7. Sales of the stock and the size of the block to be valued; and
8. The market price of stocks of corporations engaged in the same or similar line of business having their stock actively traded in a free and open market, either on an exchange or over-the-counter.

Rev. Rul. 59-60 emphasizes that the eight factors do not necessarily have equal weight and that determination of value is a matter of judgment and common sense to be arrived at after consideration of all factors.

Expanded Application of Rev. Rul. 59-60

By its express terms, Rev. Rul. 59-60 limits the factors it creates to valuations for estate and gift tax purposes. However, Rev. Rul. 65-192 extends these factors and the requirements for their consideration to determinations of fair market value of business interests of all types and for income and other tax purposes, not merely for estate and gift tax purposes.

1. Nature and History of the Business

A detailed study of the history of the corporation is needed to enable the appraiser to form an opinion of the degree of risk involved in the enterprise. This factor covers a broad area, involving degrees of stability, growth and diversity of operations, plus analyses and information that will reflect the general nature of the business: its risks, its hazards and its ability to withstand adverse economic swings.

Non-recurring items should be discounted since value has a close relation to future expectancy. At the valuation date in particular, the nature and condition of the plant facilities, the trend of sales and profitability, the depth and proficiency of both management and the labor force and the diversity of products and services must all be carefully examined as a part of the valuation process.

2. The Economic Outlook in General and the Condition of the Business

Determination of fair market value must include consideration of the outlook of the economy, in general, as well as the particular industry.

At the valuation date, the company's current and prospective degree of success in comparison with its competitors should be determined. Usually, this determination begins with an examination of financial data and a comparison of earnings. In addition, several questions should be asked: Would the public be an eager investor in the company? Is it a one-man company? Will future management be able to take over in the event of the death or retirement of a key man? Will the loss of key personnel be offset by insurance? Will the market for the company's products grow, decline or remain stable? Will the general economy sustain the company's future?

EXAMPLE

Consider one of the most prevalent factors encountered in closely held corporations — the effect the key man or "one-man" manager has on the value of the company. The loss of a key person will usually have a depressing effect upon the value of the stock. Other factors that may compensate for this loss would be the existence of trained personnel capable of continuing the business or adequate life insurance, which could be used to procure the needed managerial talent.

Often, the figures of the company itself tell a complete economic story. Consider the earnings of three different companies, all with the same total earnings in the past five years:

	Down, Inc.	Yo-Yo, Inc.	Up, Inc.
1984	$ 30,000	$ 20,000	$ 15,000
1985	24,000	24,000	17,000
1986	20,000	18,000	20,000
1987	16,000	22,000	23,000
1988	10,000	16,000	25,000
Totals	$100,000	$100,000	$100,000

Obviously, the appraiser must consider the earnings pattern in his valuation.

One way of computing the ultimate value, while still placing primary emphasis on later years, is to utilize a weighted average. This averaging method usually gives a larger multiple to the latest year (5 for 1988 in the following example) and a smaller multiple to the earlier years (for example, 3 for 1986). The computation for Down, Inc., might be as follows:

```
1984      $30,000  x 1 = $ 30,000
1985       24,000  x 2 =   48,000
1986       20,000  x 3 =   60,000
1987       16,000  x 4 =   64,000
1988       10,000  x 5 =   50,000
Totals             15    $252,000
```

$\frac{\$252,000}{15} = \$16,800$ (weighted average earnings)

A weighted average does not give the best results in all circumstances; it is only one of the many methods that can be used to emphasize most recent events.

Competition is always a key issue. For example, in the case of a small brewery, the court arrived at a low value despite high book value, good earnings and consistent dividend payments (***First Trust Co. v. U.S.***, DC Cir., 1959).

3. Book Value and Financial Condition

Computation of book value is an essential starting point for determining fair market value of stock of a closely held corporation. Book value reflects acquisition cost (less accumulated depreciation) but is not necessarily related to earning power, fair market value or even liquidating value (***Nellie I. Brown***, 25 TCM 498, 1966).

The analysis should include comparative annual balance sheets for five years before the valuation date. If possible, a balance sheet at the end of the month preceding the valuation date also should be included. Among the factors that will aid the practitioner in valuing the stock are:

a. Liquid position;
b. Gross and net book value of operating assets;
c. Working capital;
d. Long-term indebtedness;
e. Capital structure; and
f. Net worth.

Assets not essential to the operation of the business should be disclosed by an examination of current and past balance sheets. These assets may add to or detract from stock value depending on their separate value and earning power. Unquestionably, non-operating assets should be revalued at their current market prices, but the figure thus obtained, less any potential tax liability on the gain, should be added to the value determined for the operating assets and business.

Remember, balance sheets are generally stated at cost. For example, a closely held corporation carrying land on its books at cost for a number of years will probably find that the fair market value of this land has appreciated. The balance sheet should be adjusted to correct for the higher value of the land to provide a more realistic worth of the company.

Finally, if the corporation has more than one class of stock, the rights and privileges of each class should be ascertained, including voting rights and powers, dividend preferences and liquidation preferences.

4. Earnings Capacity

Potential future income of the closely held corporation is a prime factor affecting its value. In assessing this factor, the practitioner should obtain detailed income statements, preferably for five or more years. Analysis of gross income by product line, major deductions from operations, net income and taxes will enable the practitioner to form opinions regarding future profitability and value of the corporate stock.

Additional information regarding non-recurring expenses, officers' salaries, depreciation methods, substantial rental expense and historical trends with regard to sales, costs and net income should be discovered through this analysis. Non-recurring items may require adjustments to reflect normal or fair earnings, and distortions — caused by erroneous or inconsistent practices — must be "normalized." Generally, past earnings records are indicative of future expected earnings, but reliance on past history, without regard to present trends in both the company and the industry, is not conducive to a realistic valuation.

NOTES
a. For an operating company, earnings are usually the most important factor in valuation (***Kline v. Commissioner,*** 13 F2d 742, 1942), but the use of historical earnings may be misleading and must be adjusted for the trends and non-recurring items.

b. For an investment company, the fair market value of underlying assets may be more important than earnings (***William Hamm, Jr.,*** 325 F2d 934, 1964).

5. Dividend-Paying Capacity

This is seldom a significant factor since those in control of a closely held business generally will not pay dividends. Instead, they realize on their investment by taking salaries and fringe benefits that are tax deductible, as opposed to dividends that are not. The capacity to pay dividends, rather than the actual dividend payout history, is what counts.

EXCEPTION
In a reorganization (a recapitalization in particular), failure to provide dividends to newly issued stock will reduce the value of the stock substantially. Dividends must either be paid or accumulated to give the stock real value.

6. Goodwill and Other Intangibles

Following is an important portion of Rev. Rul. 59-60:

"In the final analysis, goodwill is based upon earning capacity. The presence of goodwill and its value, therefore, rests upon the excess of net earnings over and above a fair return on the net tangible assets. While the element of goodwill may be based primarily on earnings, such factors as the prestige and renown of the business, the ownership of a trade or brand name and a record of successful operations over a prolonged period in a particular locality also may furnish support for the inclusion of intangible value. (In some instances it may not be possible to make a separate appraisal of the tangible and intangible assets of the business. The enterprise has a value as an entity.) Whatever intangible values there are, which are supportable by the facts, may be measured by the amount by which the appraised value of the tangible assets exceeds the net book value of such assets."

Rev. Rul. 65-193 modified Rev. Rul. 59-60 by deleting the two sentences shown above in parentheses. In my opinion, this last ruling just does not make good sense — an industrial or commercial enterprise operating at a profit should be valued only as an entity, in most instances.

Goodwill stems from various factors, the most significant of which is favored or "excess" earnings capacity. Generally, the presence — and value— of goodwill depends on the measure of any unusually high earnings and rate of return the company enjoys. It may also be the result of a patent, an unusually acceptable product, an outstanding distribution or sales system, a location that attracts customers and so on. While it usually is not accorded a separate value, it is part of the earnings capacity and indicates a more valuable company (***Inga Bardahl**, 24 TCM 841, 1965; **Harry Trotz**, 26 TCM 632, 1967).*

Rev. Rul. 68-609 sets out a formula approach that may be used in determining the fair market value of intangible assets where there is no better basis for making the determination. Only in rare and unusual cases will the appraiser encounter circumstances that will require use of this formula approach. The analysis of the business pursuant to the other guidelines in this book will normally encompass the valuation of goodwill and intangible value.

The question that is often asked is how do you value the goodwill of a restaurant. The simple, yet absolutely correct, answer is you don't. Logic tells you goodwill can have no existence (value) aside from the business it is connected with. For example, a buyer can buy certain assets — accounts receivable, inventory or equipment — of a business without buying the entire business. No buyer would buy only the goodwill of a business without also buying the right to operate the business. More simply put, goodwill has no separate value like other tangible assets of a business.

The easiest way I know of getting a handle on how a particular value might be assigned to goodwill is to talk in terms of numbers. Let's use an example to explain the numbers.

EXAMPLE

Joe buys a restaurant for $1,000,000. The price includes all assets of the business — tangible and intangible (goodwill). The fair market value of the tangible assets (receivables, inventory and equipment) is $800,000. This means Joe paid $200,000 ($1,000,000 – $800,000) for the goodwill.

7. Sales of Stock and Size of the Block to Be Valued

Prior sales of stock are said to be the best evidence of value if the sales were close in time to the valuation date and under comparable circumstances. The problem is that prior sales usually were "forced" or "distressed" and seldom have been made under comparable circumstances and thus the courts rarely accord much weight to prior sales (***South Carolina National Bank v. McLeod, 256 FSupp** 913, 1966).*

A minority interest in a closely held corporation is harder to dispose of than a controlling interest since such an interest cannot control dividend payments or force a liquidation. The courts have historically recognized this and permitted discounts for minority interests in a closely held corporation. This is an extremely important concept and is discussed in depth in Chapter VII.

8. Market Price of Actively Traded Comparable Stocks

a. In Concept

From a conceptual standpoint, it is almost impossible to make valid comparisons of listed companies with closely held companies.

i. Where the closely held company is small, the size differential alone makes comparison impossible. In ***Russel v. U.S.** (**260 FSupp** 493, 1966),* the court said that comparison should be made with other small, not large, meat companies (***South Carolina National Bank v. McLeod,** supra*).

ii. Closely held companies often pay large salaries and expense items that a public company would capitalize. Accounting treatment may also differ.

iii. Public companies have a depth of management that closely held companies often lack.

iv. Closely held companies usually are limited to one product, while a public company that makes the same product will usually have several other lines that may or may not be related. In *Righter* (Extr. 439 F2d 1204, 1971), the court held that comparison with listed companies producing a full line of toys and games is of little significance where the closely held company produces only two adult games.

v. Public companies have access to credit lines unavailable to closely held companies.

vi. As an investor, a person might pay $100 per share for 500 shares of GM for one set of reasons; yet, that same person might pay the same $500,000 (more or less) for 100% of the stock of a closely held manufacturing company as an investor/operator for a completely different set of reasons.

b. In Practice

Blind use of comparables often produces absurd results. The example below actually happened.

EXAMPLE

A closely held company was in the retail business, and the valuation was based on 1984 data. Earnings for 1984 were 25% higher than those for 1983, and book value had increased substantially. Obviously, the company could not be worth less in 1984 than it was in 1983. The average price earnings ratios, however, for 10 listed comparable companies fell from 20.0 in 1983 to 6.7 in 1984. If the numbers produced by the mechanical use of comparables were used as the measure of value, the forced conclusion was that in 1984 the closely held company was worth only one-third of what it was worth in 1983. This result is absurd and illustrates the danger of using comparables.

CHAPTER IV

VALUATION METHODS

This chapter has been written for your professional, but you should read it to see for yourself that when you value your business for tax purposes, "getting clobbered" by the IRS need not occur.

THE EIGHT MAJOR APPROACHES TO VALUATION

It has been said that the number of different valuation approaches in existence at any point in time can be determined by multiplying all the appraisers in the world by the number of businesses to be valued.

The Most Common Approaches

Years of practice and experience have singled out the following eight approaches as the most common valuation candidates:

1. Comparative values of similar going concerns;
2. Reproduction or replacement value;
3. Present value of the cash flow;
4. Liquidation approach;
5. Book value;
6. Factor approach (often called a formula approach);
7. Earnings approach; and
8. Combinations and variations.

Observation

At this point, it should be observed that basically there are only two approaches to valuation — either the liquidation approach or the earnings approach. All other approaches are combinations.

Which is best? Which should be used and when? Actually, there is not any pat or right answer. Often, an approach that is just right under one set of circumstances would give ridiculous results if the facts were to change slightly.

1. Comparative Values of Similar Going Concerns

The most widely used method of valuation of closely held corporations entails an examination of "comparable" publicly held companies and the prices of actual transactions of securities in these companies on or near the valuation date.

The search for comparable companies might begin with industry classification. In theory, companies in the same industry share similar markets, and the potential for sales and earnings growth is usually dependent upon the characteristics of the growth rate of the market. In addition, companies in the same industry are often affected by common operating (production and supply) characteristics. Upon reviewing all those public firms in the same industry classification, revisions may be made for size, diversity, growth, stability, leverage, dividends and so on.

The rationale of this method is based on the observation that during any relatively short period of time, the relative sales prices of the public common stock within a given industry generally can be related to the stock of the closely held company. Somehow the relative investment characteristics of these giant companies and closely held businesses are supposed to be alike. I don't buy it. See my comments under "8. Market Price of Actively Traded Comparable Stocks" in Chapter III under the section titled "Expanded Application of Rev. Rul. 59-60."

In particular, this comparative approach does not make sense for any but the very largest closely held businesses. And even there it is of limited value.

2. Reproduction or Replacement Value

This is the cost it takes to replace or reproduce the facilities and systems of the business being valued, by going into the marketplace and obtaining replacement assets. This method is used for insurance purposes. Also, if the seller has unique property, something the buyer really wants in terms of a physical plant that is operating, this method may be the first choice.

3. Present Value of the Cash Flow

This approach is concerned with the value of the cash flow of the business adjusted for the time value of money and the business and economic risks. The theory is that cash flow represents the recovery of the investment and the receipt of income produced by such investment. This method contains the following factors:

a. The expected growth rates in sales and earnings projected to a selected date on which the stock may be sold.

b. The time period between the valuation date and the sale date.

c. The dividend payout of the company (as it is or potentially could be).

d. An expected price-earnings ratio or liquidation value at the end of the time frame date. A perpetual dividend stream also could be used.

e. A rate of return the investor might seek given his expectation of the four points above, less a discount for the risk of not having such expectations realized.

Cash flow is assumed to be a more valid criterion of the value than "book or accounting" profits. Only cash or cash equivalents can be used for reinvestment purposes.

This method (also called the "Discounted Cash Flow Approach" or "Investment Approach") is often used for non-tax purposes to arrive at a comparable price at which to establish an exchange ratio or in certain other circumstances — for example, a merger.

EXAMPLE

Suppose a "rational investor" decides the risk for the business he wants to buy merits a 15% return. He assumes an annual cash return of $10,000 a year for 10 years and a liquidation value of $100,000.

The value today (right now), called the "present value," is $74,840. The following schedule shows how the investor would arrive at this value.

Year	Annual Cash	+	Liquidation Value	=	Total Cash	x	Discount (15%) Factor	Present Value
1	$10,000				$ 10,000		.869	$8,690
2	10,000				10,000		.756	7,560
3	10,000				10,000		.657	6,570
4	10,000				10,000		.571	5,710
5	10,000				10,000		.497	4,970
6	10,000				10,000		.432	4,320
7	10,000				10,000		.375	3,750
8	10,000				10,000		.326	3,260
9	10,000				10,000		.284	2,840
10	10,000		$100,000		$110,000		.247	$27,170

Total Present Value $74,840

The mechanics of the above schedule are simple. If an investor had $8,690 on the first day of Year 1 and it earned 15% for a full year ($1,310), he would have $10,000 at the end of the year ($8,690 + $1,310) and so on.

To use this method you would do all things necessary to get the figures ready before using the method as illustrated above — you would project the growth of the company, adjust the book value of the balance sheet for undervalued assets, adjust expenses for items (like excess owner's salary) that distort real profits and apply the other factors discussed in this chapter.

> *HINT*
> If you use this (or any other approach), the rate of return expected would depend on what else is available in the marketplace. For example, if the market place on the day you are doing the valuation showed:

Investment Opportunity	Relative Risk	Pretax Return
Long-term U.S. Gov't. Bonds	Lowest	8%
Seasoned "Aa" Corporate Bonds	Low	9
Seasoned "Baa" Corporate Bonds	Medium	10

What rate of return would you want as a "rational investor"? The message should be clear. If you can get 8 percent or more, depending on the current market, with little or no risk, a restaurant business (with great risk) only makes sense if the rate of return rewards you for the added risk.

4. Liquidation Approach

Investment companies usually are valued on a liquidation basis. If an operating company has non-operating assets, such assets should be segregated for valuation purposes. In a like manner, the operating assets and the income produced by such assets must be valued separately.

As a practical matter, every business is worth at least liquidation value. If the operating assets — particularly fixed assets — are left in place to be used in a continuing business, then the package has a minimum value at or near reproduction or replacement cost less depreciation. Replacement cost, unless the property is unique, means fair market value.

Liquidation value of a going business can be tricky: Costs, expenses and losses must be estimated for selling the inventory, collecting receivables, terminating employees, selling off assets as no longer needed and many other winding-down activities.

5. Book Value

Among other names, this approach to valuation is called "net tangible asset value" or "adjusted book value."

Tangible book value is obtained by reference to the business' most recent balance sheet. In essence, it is the net book value of the business — total assets minus total liabilities, with adjustment made for intangibles such as goodwill.

Adjusted book value is based upon making the necessary adjustments to book value for such factors as economic depreciation of plant and equipment, appreciation of land and other real estate values, understated or overstated inventories due to accounting method, etc.

Typically, little or no judgment is required to value assets using this approach. If required, each asset on the balance sheet should be restated at fair market value.

Such a valuation can be accomplished mechanically by completing a schedule similar to the following:

Steps for Determination of Adjusted Book Value

1. Start with Book Value. $ _____
2. Add (or subtract) the necessary
   figure to arrive at line 3.   _____
3. Appraisal or fair market value
   (this would be the number for which
   all assets — like fixed assets and
   inventory — with any value could be
   sold if the company were to be
   liquidated).   _____
4. Subtract all intangibles on the
   books that have no value (that is,
   cannot be sold separately in liquidation), such as goodwill or a covenant
   not to compete.   _____
5. Balance — Adjusted Book Value. $ _____

The adjusted book value approach is important because it is one of the elements used in other valuation approaches that follow.

Book value as the sole or predominant factor also makes sense in certain special situations. For example:

1. A business that is relatively new;
2. Earnings have been unstable;
3. The sole owner is disabled or has died; or
4. An earnings approach to valuation is highly speculative. For example, uncertainty due to supply shortages, strikes, government legislation or product obsolescence makes the future unpredictable.

NOTE

Of course, to accomplish the above, appraisals may be necessary to determine the value of equipment, real estate and other items.

Obtain them.

You may want to deduct anticipated liquidation expenses if in fact the business is to be liquidated; if the business is to be continued, such deductions make no sense.

Intangibles are removed because the value of the business in excess of the tangible assets is in theory to be determined by one or more of the methods that follow.

6. Factor Approach

According to this method, three major factors have proven to be the most significant in determining value. They are: (1) earnings, (2) dividend-paying capacity and (3) book value.

Earnings are normally the prime interest of the investor, but their weight, of course, must be tempered by consideration of the type of business being valued. Companies that sell a product usually give earnings heavier weight. On the other hand, gross revenue is often the main factor in the valuation of a strictly service operation.

When an investment or a holding company is valued, the greatest weight is given to the underlying net asset values. The payment of dividends does not merit much weight in the valuation of closely held stock. Dividend payments in a closely held company are subject to a "controlled" situation and are not usually representative of what might be paid out. It is the dividend-paying capacity (as opposed to dividends actually paid) that must be considered.

The factor approach was used in two well-known cases: *Bader* (*Bader v. U.S.,* 172 FSupp. 833, 1959) and *Central Trust* (*Central Trust Co., Ext. v. U.S.,* 350 F2d 393, 1962).

The computation below shows the use of weighted averages in the determination of stock value according to a factor approach:

	Capitalized Value	Bader Weight	Bader Value	Central Trust Weight	Central Trust Value
1. Earnings: $50 x 12.5	$625	2	$1,250	.5	$312
2. Dividends: $25 x 24.0	$600	1	$600	.3	$180
3. Book Value: $800 x .6	$480	1	$480	.2	$96
4. Total		4	$2,330	1.0	$588
5. Average			$582		$588
6. Discount: 10.00 percent			$58		
12.17 percent					$72
7. Per-Share Value			$524		$516

In *Bader,* the court gave twice the weight to earnings (2) as it did to dividends and book value (1 each). The total weight (4) is divided into the total value ($2,330) to arrive at the average ($582). A similar approach is used in *Central Trust.*

IMPORTANT DISCOUNT CONCEPT INTRODUCED

The court in *Bader* used a weighted average of three factors: double weight for capitalized earnings, plus single weight for dividends and adjusted book value. That was the method of valuation. But the big news in 1959 was (and still is today) — the court allowed a discount of 10 percent for lack of marketability.

In *Central Trust,* a weighted average was used differently: 50 percent for capitalized earnings, 30 percent for dividends and 20 percent for adjusted book value. A discount of 12.17 percent was allowed for lack of marketability, and a further discount of approximately 7.5 percent for other factors (including the fact that some sales of stock had been made to employees and friends at a greatly reduced price in recent years). It is now a well-developed concept — a discount should be applied to the value of a closely held corporation due to its lack of marketability. This concept is explored in greater detail in Chapter VII.

7. Earnings Approach

The earnings approach rarely is ignored in the valuation of an operating privately held business. However, the earnings approach can yield extremely different results depending upon the purpose of the valuation and the nature of the entity to be valued. It is usually the investor's best method for calculating expected return on investment.

Judgment must be exercised at each of two significant levels when implementing the earnings approach.

At one level, the "true" earnings of the business must be determined. Adjustments must be made for such items as officers' salaries and expenses that would not be made, or if made, not in the same amount, by the usual self-serving owners of a privately held business. The number of operating years (three, four or five) to be considered, eliminated (as not representative) or weighted (with greater weight given to the most recent years) must be selected.

8. Combinations and Variations

In most valuations of an operating business, a combination of more than one basic method is employed to arrive at the final valuation. Also, the variations used are at least equal to the number of businesses to be valued. There is not one correct way (or even 101 correct ways).

The value of any particular restaurant or chain of restaurants is usually determined by using a combination of approaches. The following approach is offered, not so much as an approach to be used, but as one of many approaches that can give proper valuation results.

EXAMPLE

1. Determine the average after-tax earnings for the company for five years. $360,000

2. Determine the average annual net tangible assets used in the business for the five-year period. $2,000,000

3. Apply a fair rate of return on the average net tangible assets computed in (2). Say 15% x $2,000,000. $300,000

4. Deduct (3) from (1): equals excess earnings attributable to goodwill. $60,000

5. Capitalize the excess earnings in (4) at a selected rate to yield the value of goodwill (or intangibles). Say 25% (or a multiple of 4 x $60,000). $240,000

6. Add net tangible assets of the company as of the valuation date to (5):

    a. Assuming net tangible assets (adjusted book value) at the valuation date of $2,500,000

    PLUS

    b. Capitalized excess earnings from (5). $240,000

    c. The fair market value is $2,740,000

Voila! $2,740,000 is the fair market value — no more, no less! Ridiculous!

The mathematical result should not be the exclusive test. Remember the failure of ARM 34 (see Page 21). Every element of the business and every factor that affects it must be taken into consideration — the nature and history of the business, quality of management, future prospects, competition, general economic and industry outlook — alas! — all the rhetoric contained in this chapter, plus a liberal amount of the appraiser's gut feeling, which seems to improve with age and experience.

NOTES

1. This method can (and often does) produce a fair market value that is less than adjusted book value. Such a result is acceptable to a point. If the valuation figure dips below liquidation value (after deducting estimated liquidation expenses), then liquidation value must be used.

2. Whatever the fair market value as determined might be, an appropriate discount must be taken. See Chapter VII.

Comments Concerning the Example

STEP #1 — Determine the average after-tax earnings for the business for five years. The earnings must be analyzed and adjustments made for non-recurring items, discretionary expenses and so on. Remember, what you are trying to do is predict what the products will be in the future years by proforming out those expenses and income items that are not likely to occur again. You would proforma in anticipated future expenses and income. The example uses $360,000 for Step #1. Note again it is the average earnings after taxes.

Now a question — What earnings would you use as the average earnings if the after-tax profits of your business for the past five years were:

Year	Profit
1984	$120,000
1985	60,000
1986	20,000
1987	70,000
1988	480,000
Total	$750,000

Would you use a simple average of the above — $150,000? How about giving extra weight to the $480,000 profit of 1988? After all, it is the most recent year. My tendency, without any more facts about this specific business, would be to throw out 1988 as an extraordinary year.

STEP #2 — Determine the average annual net tangible assets used in the business for the five-year period. First convert each item on the balance sheet to its adjusted book value. For our purposes, adjusted book value of the tangible assets means fair market value. The example uses $2,000,000. Remember, this is the average of the annual net tangible assets as adjusted. You actually would have added up the net tangible assets as adjusted for each of the five years and divided by five.

STEP #3 — Apply a fair rate of return (usually 10 percent to 20 percent) on the average net tangible assets computed in Step #2. A good rule-of-thumb is to use a rate of return that is approximately two points over the prime rate of interest plus additional points for risk. In our example we use 15 percent. The fair rate of return is $300,000 (15% x $2,000,000).

STEP #4 — Deduct the number arrived at in Step #3 from the number arrived at in

Step #1. This is the excess earnings attributable to goodwill (the intangible value of the business) or, in this case, $60,000.

STEP #5 — Capitalize the excess earnings in Step #4 at a rate of from 15 percent to 50 percent. Yes, it could be higher or lower. This multiple will be higher if you have a steady old-line business and lower if you have a business that is new or tends to have widely fluctuating profits. We use 25 percent in the example, or a multiple of 4 (100 ÷ 25), resulting in $240,000 (10% is a multiple of 10; 20%, 5; 33-1/3%, 3; and so on). One more point: Uncertainty increases the risk and lowers the multiple.

STEP #6 — Add the net tangible assets at the valuation date. We use $2,500,000. Remember, in Step #2 we used the average annual net tangible assets. The figure to be used here is the value of the net tangible assets on the valuation date, not the five-year average. To that figure add the capitalized excess earnings from Step #5 or $240,000. The fair market value is precisely $2,740,000. Not a penny more or less. Nonsense!

Assuming all other factors have been considered, you should think of the figure as establishing a range. The range might be about 10 percent more or 10 percent less than that figure, subject to all the literature and all the experience that you can muster, together with a proper feeling in the gut. And finally—

Did you notice something as you went through the example? It looks objective. Right? Of course, you know that is wrong. The approach is extremely subjective. By changing any one of several assumptions, the results can be altered significantly.

Whatever your final figure, a discount must be applied as discussed in Chapter VII.

A Final Important Note

In the end, logic and common sense must prevail. Test your final number in terms of the other parties to the valuation. If it is necessary to take another look, then do so.

Remember, the courts may be the final judge. You might enjoy what one court said in a valuation case involving a disputed valuation:

> "Too often in valuation disputes the parties have convinced themselves of the unalterable correctness of their positions and have consequently failed to con-clude settlement negotiations — a process clearly more conducive to the proper disposition of disputes such as this....The result is an overzealous effort, during the course of the ensuing litigation, to infuse talismanic precision into an issue which should frankly be recognized as inherently imprecise and capable of resolution only by Solomon-like pronouncement" (***Messing v. Commissioner***, 48 TC 502).

> "...Indeed, each of the parties should keep in mind that, in the final analysis, the Court may find the evidence of valuation by one of the parties sufficiently more convincing than that of the other party, so that the final result will produce a sig-nificant financial defeat for one or the other, rather than a middle of the road compromise which we suspect each of the parties expects the Court to reach" (***Buffalo Tool & Die Mfg. Co. v. Commissioner***, 84 TC 441, 1980).

CHAPTER V

BLENDING IN YOUR FACTS

This is where we get our advantage. The facts (and I mean the "true" facts about your restaurant business) blended with the law tip the valuation scale in your favor.

FACT, NOT LAW, DETERMINES VALUE

The law is tough enough when you try to value a closely held company. If you fail to get all the *facts,* applying even *good law to wrong or incomplete facts* will almost always cause a tax disaster. Awareness of the guidelines set forth in Rev. Rul. 59-60 and the cases thereunder can do no harm, but legal guidelines alone are not sufficient. The valuation battle is won in the preparation, not on appeal. Look first, and look hard, at the company or business to be valued.

Valuation experience continues to teach us that each company to be valued has its own set of facts and circumstances, and each valuation is unique and different from every other valuation. Two companies in similar lines of business with almost identical numbers can have quite different values because of one significant fact difference. No set of textbook rules can bring out the importance of unique facts.

HOW TO GET STARTED

Every valuation must commence with an examination of the balance sheet and operating statement. But care must be taken to recognize that both are nothing but sets of numbers. It is important to distinguish between numbers and facts. Numbers represent historical earnings, margins, return on equity, book value and so on. Numbers are precise and, if correct, are tough to argue — either for or against.

On the other hand, facts are the reasons behind the numbers. Facts are not self-evident from a mere reading of the numbers. Facts have to be dug out, verified, assessed and often discarded for lack of weight. Facts are found everywhere, and the search for them must go everywhere.

Numbers can have a fatal attraction in the valuation process because by their nature they are self-quantifying. Being wholly mathematical, numbers lend themselves all too easily by arithmetic process to translation into the valuation figure, which is also a number. Numbers alone may be easy to work with, but to produce easy answers or quick answers is not to produce sound answers.

Your job, or the job of the appraiser you hire, is to blend the numbers and the facts into a valuation that will withstand attack from the IRS. In order to succeed, you need an organized way to gather the facts. The following checklists will do just that.

FACT-GATHERING CHECKLISTS

A. Balance Sheet
To arrive at "adjusted book value," examine the balance sheet in detail.
1. Inventory
Test the quality of the inventory, particularly wine and liquor. Is it LIFO or FIFO? A LIFO inventory may have one value for going concern purposes (requiring an adjustment to arrive at adjusted book value) and another value for liquidation purposes.
2. Receivables
Test the aging and the quality of receivables. Failure to write off bad debts means earnings are overstated.
3. Assets Not Essential to the Operations of the Business
Assets such as securities or real estate that are not used in the business or will not be used in future expansion should be valued separately at fair market value. The value determined for these assets should be added as a separate item to the value of the operating portion of the business. Operating earnings should also be adjusted for

earnings contributions from such non-essential assets.

4. Real Estate

If you have had any real estate (used in the operations of the business) on the books for a long period of time, the depreciated value is probably well under its market value. Remember, the operating portion of the business may have little or no value without the real estate. For example, the cost of moving may be prohibitive, or a key factor in the restaurant's success is its location.

5. Tangible Personal Depreciable Property

Should equipment and other such assets be adjusted to fair market value (usually called appraisal value at this initial stage)? If it is a non-operating asset (decor items or works of art) or an asset no longer to be used in operations, the answer is clearly "Yes!" But if the asset is used in operations, the answer usually must await further probing; increasing the value of the asset requires an upward adjustment of future depreciation. The increased appraisal value raises the ultimate fair market value, while the increased depreciation lowers future book profits and the ultimate value — one works against the other. Similar reasoning says that if a particular piece of equipment is worth more right now, future earnings will be reduced because of the increased cost of replacing that equipment when it wears out or becomes obsolete — more circular reasoning.

Quite often, even though tangible personal property is worth substantially more than book value, no adjustment is made for valuation purposes. Nevertheless, the problem, if applicable, should be recognized in the appraisal report.

TAX ON APPRECIATED ASSETS

Federal income and other taxes that would be incurred in liquidating underlying assets at appraised values are among the "costs" that should be considered. Book value should only be adjusted upward to the net appreciated fair market value, after taxes, for non-operating assets. Appreciated assets that are used in the operation of the business, unless there is an intent to sell the asset in the near future, should not be reduced by anticipated taxes that would be due on sale.

6. Age, Nature and Efficiency of the Restaurant's Facilities Will Dictate Its Sales, Earnings and Dividends Capacity

Facilities used efficiently, but with additional capacity, suggest the potential for growth without substantial spending. If the facilities are operating at, or close to, full capacity, further growth will dictate additional spending and financing.

7. Intangible Property

Intangible property (usually purchased goodwill or the right to use a name) either should be eliminated (because it has no intrinsic value) or adjusted to appraisal value as circumstances require.

8. Leasehold Improvements

On liquidation these are usually worth nothing; for a going concern, book value is usually used.

9. Loans to Shareholders

Are they collectible or worthless?

10. Loans from Shareholders

Is this debt or equity? How would someone purchasing the assets and assuming the liabilities treat this item?

B. Operating Statement

If you use any valuation approach involving earnings, the operating statement must be analyzed. Appropriate statements (increasing or decreasing profit) must be made for each year of operations being considered.

    1. Salaries of Owners

    If salaries are excessive, earnings are understated.

    2. Depreciation

    If accelerated methods are used, earnings may be understated, but the opposite will be true when acceleration runs out. Additional and immediate requirements for capital expenditures might have greater impact than past or anticipated future depreciation.

    3. LIFO Reserve

    If you adjust to FIFO basis (unrealistic because you cannot shift back and forth), you increase not only earnings, but also inventory and equity, which ruins the balance sheet. Usually this is a futile exercise, but you should be aware of it.

    4. Extraordinary Items

    Sale of land, equipment or a division may generate a profit or loss, the effect of which should be eliminated since this does not represent normal business operations.

    5. Unusual Year

    A year of abnormally high profit or loss should be excluded unless other circumstances indicate a recurring trend.

    6. Non-operating Assets

    Exclude income and expenses from portfolios, rental real estate and so on if they are not part of normal operations.

    7. Earnings Trends

    If earnings are erratic, average them; if rising or falling, you may want to weight the later years, but you should investigate the reasons. Consider the effect of such items as an increase in the minimum wage on projected earnings.

    8. Employee Benefit Contribution

    If the company is to be sold to a buyer who has a benefit plan different from the seller's plan, adjust earnings up or down as required.

C. Intangibles

    1. Some factors exercise either a positive or negative effect on the value of goodwill. They are:

        a. Favorable location;

        b. Reputation for quality, service or special foods or beverages;

        c. Low prices;

        d. Business doesn't keep up with changing market conditions;

        e. Location is vital to success, but occupancy of location is not assured by lease or ownership; and

        f. Depends on personality or special skills of an individual who will not be available after the business is acquired. If the owner goes, so does the goodwill. Items (a) and (b) are positive; the others are negative.

    2. Other intangible assets, if they do exist, should be valued separately from the goodwill. They include:

        a. Right to use a name and

        b. Covenant not to compete.

D. Determine the answers to the following questions:

    1. If the company is a corporation:

        a. Have dividends been paid? When and how much?

        b. Does the corporation pay directors' fees? How much and how often?

    2. Are there any outstanding loans to/from the company from the shareholders and/or partners? Do these transactions represent valid obligations of the borrower?

    3. Have there been any extraordinary items in the last five years that would account

for an unusual fluctuation in earnings (i.e., fire, flood, gain on sale of non-operating assets, bad weather in a seasonal resort area)?

4. How does the company determine bad debts? Are there any bad debts that need to be written off?

5. Who has legal ownership of the major operating assets, usually land and building? If the assets are in individuals' names as opposed to the company's name, what are the future plans for these assets?

6. What is the depreciation policy of the company for tax purposes and for reporting purposes? Is there any equipment carried at zero cost or at a cost significantly lower than replacement cost? Conversely, is any relatively new equipment carried at a high cost, yet is really obsolete?

7. What is the exact valuation date? What are the objectives of the client?

8. Has the business ever been valued before? (If so, obtain a copy.)

E. Here is a basic list of documents and data to gather:

1. Tax returns for the company for the last five years.

2. Financial statements for the last five years (both income statements and balance sheets).

3. Detail of company's ownership:

    a. Partnership-partners — capital and profits interest and cost basis of their interest.

    b. Corporation-shareholders — stockholdings and cost basis of their stock.

4. Detail of officers' compensation for the preceding five years and the percentage of time the officers devoted to the business.

5. Current real estate appraisals.

6. Copies of significant long-term agreements such as franchise agreements, leases of major assets, etc.

7. Information on the existing economic conditions of the area/industry, such as publications of the local Chamber of Commerce.

8. Volume of sales by location if more than one unit.

9. Projections prepared for the next year, or, if available, for as many years as done.

10. A copy of the company's long-range plan or strategic plan.

> **HINT**
> Use the checklists every time you value your business. Add points to the list as required. However, using checklists does not automatically produce answers. Often, for any given case, only one or two points on the checklist may be relevant. When a bell rings, research and evaluate the relevant point thoroughly.

EXAMPLES — WHY NUMBERS ALONE CAN FOOL YOU

The following real-life examples were deliberately selected to illustrate the importance of going beyond the mere numbers that appear on the balance sheet and the operating statement. In each case, the numbers alone would have indicated a different value, which in some cases would have been dramatically different.

> **NOTE**
> The nature of the businesses — manufacturing, retail and restaurant — in the examples are not as important as the concepts illustrated.

Example 1
A federal estate tax return had already been filed indicating a value of $1.1 million

for a manufacturing company whose steady earnings were consistent with the $1.1 million value. Before IRS audit, the value was questioned by the estate, and the facts were re-examined. Inspection of the building revealed severe physical deterioration and an admission by management that the building was on the condemned list; plans had been made to acquire a new, more expensive plant elsewhere. Figures were developed on the cost of the new building, the out-of-pocket expense of the move, and the salvage value of the old building. This produced a net cost of $0.5 million for the move. On audit — with the IRS — it was pointed out that while the historical earnings justified a value of $1.1 million, no buyer would pay that amount knowing another $0.5 million would be required to move the facility. The estate argued that a buyer would pay only $0.6 million ($1.1 million – $0.5 million). With some minor adjustment, that figure was accepted by the IRS.

Example 2

A retail clothing store had, in the most recent five-year period preceding the death of the owner, doubled its sales and earnings. These facts gave the initial impression that the company was doing far better than average and that it should be valued at a higher multiple than normal. This impression was erroneous. In each year the store space had been expanded, net sales per square foot were unchanged from year one to year five. The owner had doubled his investment to double his sales and earnings. A buyer would have to increase his investment beyond what he paid at the valuation date if he wished to increase his sales and earnings. Thus, the impression that the historic five-year growth would continue automatically in the hands of a buyer and warrant paying a premium for the business vanished.

Example 3

The decedent held the stock of a corporation that owned a building and a small parcel of land from which a restaurant business was conducted. The decedent also held the beneficial interest in a land trust that owned a large parking lot adjacent to and leased by the restaurant. One person (a real estate appraiser) valued the parking lot at $70,000.

Another person looked at the numbers for the restaurant and valued it at $400,000. By simple addition, the value of the two holdings equaled $470,000. Subsequently, it was pointed out that the restaurant was worth $400,000 only if the parking lot was available. If no parking lot had been available, the restaurant would be out of business and worth only salvage value. The IRS accepted the no-value-to-the-parking-lot approach and agreed to a $400,000 value for the two holdings.

Example 4

The decedent had been a member of a very small group that had for years owned and operated a successful manufacturing company. When the lawyers, accountants and advisers prepared to value the decedent's interest in the corporation, it was under the assumption that the decedent's 60 percent interest was represented by common stock. Then, someone suddenly remembered that the decedent did not own common stock, but a voting trust certificate entitling the holder to receive 60 percent of the common stock upon expiration of the voting trust some eight years after date of death. A holder of a voting trust certificate has no voice in running the corporation; this power resides in the voting trustee. Despite the nominal representation of 60 percent control, the voting trust certificate holder has no more voice in management than the holder of a minority interest. This argument was made to the IRS and resulted in a 25 percent discount from the full value of 60 percent of the stock of the corporation. The most important valuation factor in this example had nothing to do with the numbers but rather with the discovery of the precise nature of the interest in the company held by the decedent.

CHAPTER VI

MUST CONSIDERATIONS WHEN VALUING YOUR RESTAURANT

You will discover that logic, added to the facts, brings the IRS' "rules of valuation" into the range of reason.

This is one of the shortest chapters in the book. Yet, it is the most important. Why? It is the peculiar nature of our industry — the restaurant industry.

Step back for a moment and look at the industry (the forest) as a whole. Then, you can better see the particular segment (the trees) in which you operate. This will allow you to get a better look at how your individual business (your tree) fits into the picture! As the entire forest can be ravaged by fire, storm and disease, so can our industry be ravaged by outside forces. Sometimes only a limited area of the forest (like a certain market area or niche) is totally destroyed or severely damaged. Forests grow back. So do businesses. But in the meantime, the value all but disappears.

Simply put, a healthy tree in a diseased forest has limited value. So does a thriving business in a sick economy. Let's face it, our industry has been, is today and probably always will be like the sphere on a yo-yo — going up and down. Sometimes the market forces doing the pulling and pushing are easy to identify: the national economy; inflation; and the economy and growth of your local market area. These will do for starters. No doubt you can add to the list for your particular business or market niche.

It's a fact. Any one of these market forces can either skyrocket the value of your business or stuff your life's work down a tube overnight. Sometimes these market forces work in tandem to create overnight millionaires (seldom) or instant bankruptcies (more often than should be the case). It is the job of the appraiser to identify two aspects of these market forces. First, if market forces are currently affecting your industry, market niche or individual business, is the impact positive or negative?...How much will it affect your business?...for how long? Second and much tougher, if identifiable market forces are not affecting your business now, what is the likelihood of these forces striking in the foreseeable future?

This chapter will help you identify some of the forces — market and otherwise — that might affect the value of your business. If I have some thoughts on what can be done to mitigate negative forces or enhance positive forces, I'll put in my two cents worth.

Specific and Unique Apply to Every Business

Every business has its own peculiarities. The first order of business to valuing a business is to accumulate the facts and data listed in Chapter V. This must be done no matter what type of business is being valued. Then, you must get very specific by accumulating information relating to the unique factors and forces that apply to the business being valued in the specific industry in which the business operates — in our case, restaurant businesses.

Now let's take a look at the specific factors and forces you should consider today to help make your business more valuable tomorrow.

Your Position in the Marketplace

Consumers — both businesses and individuals — require goods and services. As simplistic as it sounds, it is imperative that you monitor the economic winds. The general demand for goods and services in good economic times causes almost all restaurants to be more profitable during such periods. Simple! And everyone knows it. So what.

Unless your business is going against the tide, your business is worth more in good times than in bad.

A MONEY-MAKING AND TAX-SAVING HINT

For those of you who will someday sell your business rather than transfer it to a family member, get your business valued and sell it in good times. DO NOT SELL AT

THE BOTTOM OF THE CYCLE.

On the other hand, it makes more sense to transfer your business to your family in bad times. The value is low and you can beat the tax collector legitimately.

CHECKLIST OF BASIC QUESTIONS ABOUT YOUR RESTAURANT THAT AFFECT VALUE

1. <u>Loss of Key Personnel</u>

Is there backup management? Can key people be replaced? What would be the impact on your business if one or more key people were lost? Will life insurance solve the problem until new people can be trained?

2. <u>Present Facility</u>

Is it condemned? Is it adequate for near-term, or will it have to be enlarged or replaced? Is the lease about to expire? How will the cost of these affect future earnings? Can the business survive a move?

3. <u>State of Your Specific Market Niche</u>

If static, what is the possibility of future growth for your restaurant? What is the impact of present governmental — both federal and local — regulations, the likelihood of new or changed regulations? Will specialty food products be in short supply so as to put you out of business or cause profits to rise because you have a source; or could it be the other way around, with the market being flooded by an oversupply, killing profit margins?

4. <u>Competition Affecting Your Immediate Market</u>

Are you gaining or losing customers for any of the usual competitive reasons? If so, do you have a plan to stop losses or enhance gains?

5. <u>Cash Flow</u>

Will business requirements outrun your cash flow because of:

    a. Inability to pay debt?

    b. Needed capital investments?

    c. Inflation?

    d. Inability to obtain additional financing?

6. <u>Market Area</u>

Is your market area growing? Shrinking? Do you get an adequate rate of growth when the market area grows?

7. <u>Location</u>

What is your proximity to major highways and arterial streets? Is ingress and egress for customers easy? Can layout be improved? Are major repairs required? At what cost?

8. <u>Neighborhood</u>

Is the area going downhill? Enough to drive off customers? Make it difficult to hire employees? Increase expenses for repairs (from vandalism) and watch service?

9. <u>Equipment</u>

Must it be replaced? Repaired? At what cost?

10. <u>Basic Costs</u>

Can you maintain food costs at their present level? Are they likely to increase? Decrease? What about beverage costs? Labor costs?

11. <u>Real Estate</u>

Must the real estate be part of the package to be sold? Can you lease it to the buyer? At what rental? Is the real estate likely to appreciate?

12. <u>Liquor License</u>

Does a liquor license have value in your community? If so, is it transferable to the buyer? If not, can the buyer get a new license and at what cost?

The list could go on forever. The key is to learn to ask the right questions under the particular fact circumstances when a real-life restaurant must be valued. The best bet — hire someone who knows the restaurant industry. He'll know the right questions to ask.

A REAL-LIFE EXAMPLE

I can think of no better way to end this chapter than with a real-life example. The following letter was sent to me by a new client. As you read it, you will see point after point that affects the valuation of the business. The letter is an exact quote. All words that might identify the owner or the business, or that do not affect the valuation, are omitted. All words in parentheses were added to help clarify the words omitted.

"The Company was founded twenty-five years ago...In January 1982...all (companies) were rolled into one S Corporation. The reason behind this move at the time was to relieve the exposure to an accumulation of earnings tax, and to try to move more assets out of the Corporation for estate planning.

"The...sole stockholder is now (60) years old, married with four children...The third child is expected (to) enter the family business in about two years. The three daughters...show no interest in joining the business...wife has never been active in the business.

"The Company seems to be wallowing in mediocrity since... the late seventies.

"In spite of all the above, the Company consistently shows a bottom line profit each year with no sales growth. Operating profits are realized mainly because the Corporation has a) no debt service cost, b) little or no depreciation expenses as most of the equipment has been fully depreciated, c) (a) building...owned by (the) Corporation, completely paid, so no rental expense is charged against income....Interest from accumulated earnings further enhanced the bottom line, particularly during periods of high interest rates.

"...reluctance to plow more money into the business for new equipment and expanded facilities can probably be laid to the uncertainty of management succession and the lack of a burning desire for any greater personal income than he (the owner) already enjoys.

"...Any minority interest in the Corporation...son acquired through gift or stock option should have a restriction that the Company has the right to repurchase it at the fair market value if he leaves the Company or dies."

CHAPTER VII

HOW TO DISCOUNT YOUR VALUATION TO SAVE TAXES

The IRS does not like what the courts have done. You will love it.

The first part of this book discussed how to determine the fair market value of a closely held business. In most cases, the final value determined by using the various valuation methods and approaches discussed is not the final value that will be used by the appraiser. A further adjustment is needed to reach the final *real* fair market value that reflects the unique position of a closely held business. This adjustment is called a discount. The initial valuation figure must almost always be discounted to reflect the fact that an interest in a closely held business cannot be sold as easily as the stock of a publicly traded corporation.

THE REAL FAIR MARKET VALUE

In order to value any business for tax purposes, two distinct steps are required:
First
Value the business using the factors and approaches set out in the first part of this book and
Second
Subtract an appropriate discount from the value determined in the first step in order to arrive at the *real fair market value*. The real fair market value is the number that will be submitted to the IRS, court or other entity. There are two discounts that should be considered:
1. Discount for general lack of marketability and
2. Discount for minority interest.

SIZE OF DISCOUNT

Once it has been determined that a discount is in order, how big should it be? When negotiating a sale, a buyer will shoot for a higher discount, and the seller a lower one, if any. In tax disputes, the IRS will attempt to downplay the discount issue, while the taxpayer might use a discount to directly reduce the valuation and his taxes.

DISCOUNT FOR GENERAL LACK OF MARKETABILITY

Here is a simple way to illustrate the concept of discounting a valuation figure because of a general lack of marketability of shares of a closely held corporation. Consider a stack of stock certificates representing shares in a publicly traded corporation — such as IBM, Chrysler and Amoco. The morning paper gives yesterday's stock market value at $1,000,000. A call to your broker will bring $1,000,000, less commissions, in cold cash in four business days.

Same scene — but now take $1,000,000 worth of your Restaurant, Inc., stock just valued by the appropriate methods described in this book. Worth $1,000,000? Well, maybe. Somebody out there...when found...will pay the million...over maybe five to seven years...plus interest at 10 percent maybe, on the unpaid balance. No way is the $1,000,000 of your Restaurant, Inc., stock going to bring a real million dollars in cash or equivalent on the valuation date. Intuition tells you a discount is in order. Why and how much? That is the subject of the rest of this chapter.

The justification for a discount for a lack of marketability was stated by the court in *Central Trust* as follows:
"It seems clear...that an unlisted closely held stock of a corporation such as Heekin, in which trading is infrequent and which therefore lacks marketability, is less attractive than a similar stock which is listed on an exchange and has ready

access to the investing public."

Besides a general lack of marketability, shares of privately held corporations can be rendered unmarketable because of various restrictions on their sale or transfer.

Recent valuation cases provided substantial discounts to the stock's value for non-marketability and other inhibiting factors. In *Estate of Arthur F. Little, Jr.*, TCM 1982-26, the Tax Court allowed a total discount of 60 percent for shares of restricted stock of a publicly held company. The court allowed a 35 percent discount for sales restrictions, a 15 percent discount for an irrevocable two-year voting proxy agreement and a 10 percent discount for shares that were held in escrow.

In *William T. Piper, Sr. Est.*, 72 TC 88, the court allowed a total discount of 64 percent for stock of a corporation that owned publicly traded securities and rental property. The court allowed (1) a discount of 35 percent for lack of marketability, (2) 17 percent for relatively unattractive investment portfolios and (3) another 12 percent for possible stock registration costs.

The IRS considers the discount for lack of marketability as only one factor to be considered in valuing a business. The IRS frowns upon the use of arbitrary discount percentages (Rev. Rul. 77-287).

DISCOUNT FOR MINORITY INTERESTS

The definition of a minority interest is control of less than 50 percent of the shares of a corporation.

The discount for a minority interest in a closely held business results from the unenviable position of the minority shareholder. The holder of 15 percent (or any other minority interest) of the stock of a closely held corporation cannot determine the dividend he will get, cannot get hired at a salary of his choosing, cannot complete a sale of the corporation, plus a series of other unfortunate "cannots." Most importantly, he is helpless if he wants to cash in his 15 percent interest in the corporation. Obviously, no buyer will pay him 15 percent of the total value of the whole corporation for his interest because the buyer would be under the same disability. It necessarily follows that in the marketplace, this 15 percent interest cannot be sold for a price equivalent to 15 percent of the intrinsic value of the whole corporation. Normally, it will bring only some reduced price. Such a reduced price represents a discount.

To summarize, the minority shareholder's problem is threefold:
1. His interest lacks liquidity — The minority shareholder can get out of his position only if (a) the company goes public, (b) the business is sold or merged or (c) he sells his shares to either the company or a fellow stockholder.
2. His interest lacks current yield — Most privately held businesses don't declare dividends, and the minority shareholder is powerless to compel them.
3. His interest lacks control — The minority shareholder is powerless to affect the management and operations of the business. His interests are at the mercy of the majority shareholder.

THE SIZE OF THE MINORITY DISCOUNT

1. The IRS
The Internal Revenue Service's position toward minority discounts is stingy, as is to be expected. While conceding that the discount is usually appropriate, the IRS almost always attempts to reduce its size. And in Rev. Rul. 81-253 it refuses to allow minority

discounts for gift tax purposes when privately held stock is gifted between family members and the family as a whole owns a controlling interest. This position is at odds with court decisions that allow minority discounts in intrafamily transfers of privately held stock.

2. Historical Position of the Courts

No one, including the courts, has ever questioned the validity of the theory that a minority interest, or any interest subject to a market disability, must be discounted in value. The dispute always arises over the size of the discount. Historically, the discounts granted by the courts almost invariably have been in a low range of 5 percent to 15 percent.

3. Now the Courts Are Yielding

In the past few years the courts have tended to recognize higher discounts.

a. Discounts of 40 percent to 50 percent, once unheard of, have been granted. (See "Minority Discounts Beyond Fifty Percent Can Be Supported," 59 *Taxes* 97, February 1981, and "Nonmarketability Discounts Should Exceed Fifty Percent," 59 *Taxes* 25, January 1981, both articles by George Arneson.)

b. In *Rhoades v. U.S.* (U.S. Dist. Ct., So. Dist. Fla., 1973), a block of over-the-counter stock was so heavily burdened with the restrictions on sale that the court held it had "no ascertainable value." Because this was an income tax case, the practical effect was to value the stock at zero. The IRS did not appeal.

c. Even a government witness employed a discount of 50 percent (for illiquidity) as did the taxpayer's witness (*Estate of Ernest E. Kilpatrick,* 34 TCM 1490, 1975).

d. In *Estate of Bright* (658 F2d 999, CA-5, 1981), the court refused to value a half interest in a controlling block of 55 percent of a privately held corporation as half of a controlling interest, ruling instead that it was a 27.5 percent minority interest.

e. In *Estate of Andrews* (79 TC 938, 1982), the court applied both a discount for lack of control (minority interest) and for lack of marketability despite the fact that all shares of a privately held business were held by a decedent and his brothers. Citing the *Bright* case, the *Andrews* court held that a decedent's shares should not be valued as though the only hypothetical "willing buyer" would be a family member. To say that the only market for the decedent's shares would be a family member would violate the rule of Reg. 20.2031-1(b) regarding hypothetical willing buyers and sellers.

f. And finally, here's a case we can all applaud. The Ninth Circuit Court of Appeals let it be known that only legislation would change its position on intra-family minority discounts (*Propstra v. U.S.,* 82-2 USTC 13,475, CA-9, 1982): "...we are unwilling to impute to Congress an intent to have 'ownership of unity' principles apply to property valuations for estate tax purposes....fair market value (is defined) as the price at which property would change hands between a willing buyer and a willing seller, neither being under any compulsion to buy or sell and both having reasonable knowledge of relevant facts. By no means is this an explicit directive from Congress to apply the unity of ownership principles to estate valuations. In comparison, Congress has made explicit its desire to have unit of ownership or family attribution principles to apply in other areas of Federal tax law. In the absence of similarly explicit directives in the estate tax area, we shall not apply these principles   when computing the value of assets in the decedent's estate...."

"Defining fair market value without reference to a hypothetical willing-buyers and willing-sellers provides an objective standard by which to measure value...The use of an objective standard avoids the uncertainties that would otherwise be inherent if valuation methods attempted to account for the likeli hood that estates, legatees, or heirs would sell their interests together with others who hold undivided interests in the property. Executors will not have to make delicate inquiries into the feelings, attitudes, and anticipated behavior of those holding undivided interests in the property in question. Without an explicit direction from Congress we cannot require executors to make such inquiries.

"Not only would these inquiries require highly subjective assessments, but they might well be boundless. In order to determine whom the legatee or heir might collaborate with when selling his or her property interest, one would have to consider all the owners."

NOTE
Letter Ruling 7834004 is helpful. The IRS okayed a 30 percent discount.

MINORITY INTEREST VS. LACK OF MARKETABILITY

Courts have a tendency to lump the discount for lack of marketability and the discount for minority interest together. And in practice, that is usually what happens when a business is bought and sold. Both discounts deal in lack of marketability, but for different reasons. The discount for minority interest is concerned with the minority shareholder's lack of control over the corporation's affairs. The discount for lack of marketability is concerned with the marketability of shares of a privately held business as compared with a comparable publicly traded corporation. However, the discount for lack of marketability applies to both minority and majority (controlling) interests in the corporation.

Some courts still make a distinction between the two discounts. The Tax Court distinguished the two as follows:

In their argument neither petitioner (taxpayer) nor respondent (IRS) clearly focuses on the fact that two conceptually distinct discounts are involved here, one for the lack of marketability and the other for lack of control. The minority shareholder discount is designed to reflect the decreased value of shares that do not convey control of a closely held corporation. The lack of marketability discount, on the other hand, is designed to reflect the fact that there is no ready market for shares in a closely held corporation. Although there may be some overlap between these two discounts in that lack of control may reduce marketability, it should be borne in mind that even controlling shares in a non-public corporation suffer from lack of marketability because of the absence of a ready private placement market and the fact that flotation costs would have to be incurred if the corporation were to publicly offer its stock.

The IRS is wary of making a distinction between the two discounts because it thinks that multiple discounts result in a larger overall total discount percentage. It tells its appeals officers to use a lower capitalization rate in the valuation process to reflect any appropriate discount or discounts. Remember, the lower the capitalization rate, the higher the multiple; the higher the multiple, the higher the value. (See *IRS Valuation Guide for Income, Estate and Gift Taxes,* Federal Estate and Gift Tax Reporter (CCH), No. 115, Part II, October 14, 1985, p. 86.)

The size of lack of marketability discounts on the average is smaller than those for minority interests. This is because the courts feel that in many instances a lack of marketability can be remedied, through a public flotation offering, for example, while a minority interest has no way of improving itself short of conversion to a controlling interest through the purchase of additional stock.

The IRS considers the determination of the size of a discount an arbitrary process that is subject to dispute, just like the overall process of valuing the closely held business. One school of thought holds that an appraiser should expect that any discount percentage will be disputed by the IRS. To counter this, as in any bargaining position, the appraiser should aim high, but no higher than reason will support, with discount percentages in expectation of such a dispute. I believe in another school of thought: Take the discount that the facts and circumstances call for, then fight like a tiger for your position if the IRS dares to challenge.

PLANNING TO MAXIMIZE THE DISCOUNT AND MINIMIZE THE TAX COST — RESTAURANT OWNERS PAY HEED

Now, here is a planning technique to maximize the discount and minimize the tax cost. Get yourself into a minority position. You will solve all kinds of estate tax and other tax valuation problems. Transfer a portion of your stock to some friendly folks — like your wife or children — or consider trusts for their benefit where the trustee is independent, but thinks like you do.

CHAPTER VIII

OTHER THINGS YOU SHOULD KNOW

Valuation results can be affected by other rules and factors.

LEGAL RESTRICTIONS ON SALE OF STOCK

The commonly used methods of valuing closely held stock may go out the window wherever, by virtue of a provision in the bylaws or other agreements involving the stockholder, the owner (whether the original owner, executor or any other successor) is restricted in selecting a market for the sale of the stock. Such restrictions are found in buy-sell agreements, options and restrictive sale agreements.

Buy-Sell Agreements

This is an agreement between the corporation or an individual to buy and a stockholder to sell shares at a specified price upon death of the stockholder. Usually, the stockholder further agrees not to sell during life, except at the specified price to either the corporation or the other stockholders. Because there are mutual promises, the agreement may be enforced, and the owner cannot sell the shares except to one or more of the other contracting parties at the specified price. The courts therefore adopt the specified price as the federal estate tax value (*Estate of O.B. Littick,* 31 TC 181, 1958).

Options

This is where another person has an option to buy the stockholder's stock at a specified price on the happening of a contingency. In theory, this should fix the value just as a buy-sell agreement does because if the option is still outstanding and enforceable, the stock could not be sold to anyone for more than the option price. The courts make an important distinction, however:

1. If there was no consideration for the option, the option price is ignored for purposes of valuations (*Bensel, Edith M.,* 100 F2d 639, 1938).
2. But where consideration does exist, making the option enforceable, the option price controls for federal estate tax purposes (*Lomb v. Sugden,* 82 F2d 166, 1936).
3. Note then, an option price only sets an upper limit on value. Even if the stock could be sold for more, if the option is enforceable, the option price will control. Control the case where the stock is not worth the option price. Here you argue the optionee would not exercise his option and attempt to prove a lower value by normal means.
4. Note also the importance of both buy-sell and option agreements of a provision preventing the stockholder from selling to others during life. Absence of this provision would allow the stockholder to sell at a higher price to others before the contingency (death) happens. Therefore, the agreed price does not control (*Estate of J. H. Matthews,* 3 TC 525, 1944).

Restrictive Sale Agreements

This is where the stockholder agrees that, if the stock is to be sold during life or after death, it will first be offered at a specified price to the other stockholders or the corporation. Under such circumstances, the courts hold that the agreed price does not control (*City Bank Farmer's Trust Co.,* 23 BTA 663, 1931).

IMPORTANT HINT

One of the significant objectives of a buy-sell agreement for a closely held corporation is to fix the value of the shares owned for estate tax purposes. To attain this objective:

1. Do make the life price the same as the death price.
2. Do not use a right of the first refusal requiring a first offer to the other stockholders at a specified price (restrictive sales agreement). Why?...Because, if the other stockholders refuse to buy, the stock could then be sold at a higher price

to some third party prior to death of the seller. The same objective can be accomplished by (a) giving the remaining stockholders (and/or the corporation) an enforceable option to purchase during life and (b) at death making the purchase by the remaining stockholders (and/or the corporation) mandatory.

GOING CONCERN VALUE/GOODWILL

As if goodwill (see Chapter III under "6. Goodwill and Other Intangibles") is not enough of a monster, the courts have cooked up a new animal called "going concern value." Tax court decisions within recent years regarding going concern value have compounded confusion in an already chaotic situation.

What Is Going Concern Value?

The courts generally seem agreed that an element called "going concern value," separate from goodwill, exists. However, the courts have not been much help with how it should be valued.

The term "going concern value" was defined by the Supreme Court in 1983 (*Los Angeles Gas & Electric Corp.*, 289 U.S. 287). This case was referred to in a more recent case (*Northern Natural Gas*, 470 F2d 1107, 1973). The court said, "...there is an element of value in an assembled and established plant, doing business and earning money over one not thus advanced, and that this element of value is a property right which should be considered in determining the value of the property upon which the owner has a right to make a fair return."

Going concern value, like goodwill, is an intangible asset. It may exist with a separate value for the assemblage of a business regardless of the business profitability. For valuation purposes, going concern value must be measured separately from other assets, although it is not a property that may be sold separately. Going concern value, like goodwill, however, cannot exist or have value unless considered as part of an operating business.

Maybe the best way to identify going concern value is to set down the elements that are included in its identity:
1. The physical assets (and identifiable intangibles) of an assembled (and operating) business.
2. Non-capital costs directly related to the assembling of the business assets.
3. Even if there is no history of excess profits, it can exist. Goodwill, however, cannot exist if there is not current excess profit or potential for same in the immediate future.

Examples of Going Concern Value Would Be:
1. Start-up expenses incurred.
2. Assembled plan, management, employees and the like.
3. Assembled identifiable intangibles, such as patents and licenses.
4. Developed procedures, methods and systems that are in operation.
5. Financial and other relationships established to make the business operate.
6. Marketing, advertising and promotion concepts that are in use.
7. Sources of established supply and contracts for same.

Goodwill, on the other hand, relates to such things as the (1) physical assets (location); (2) excess profits on invested capital; and (3) kinds of things that generate continued patronage (reputation, special skills, name quality); and (4) has no existence if there are no excess profits or potential for same in the near future.

Like it or not, both the courts and the IRS have made it clear that going concern value is a new factor that must be considered (*Concord Control, Inc. v. Commissioner*, 35 TCM 1345, 1976; *VGS Corporation v. Commissioner*, 68 TC 47, 1977).

For example, in *Concord* the court held that a buyer of a business acquired a non-depreciable going concern value equal to (a) 10 percent of the purchase price of the building and (b) 20 percent of the purchase price of the machinery and equipment, tools, dies, office equipment and fixtures. This was true even though the business had no goodwill.

A WORD ABOUT THE IRS AND POSSIBLE PENALTIES

The Tax Reform Act of 1984 gives the IRS a new club to punish taxpayers who might misvalue property — including a closely held business.

Valuation Overstatements

If your income tax bill is underpaid (Section 6659) by $1,000 or more because of an overvaluation of property, you can be hit with a penalty. The overvaluation must be 150 percent or more, greater than the value finally determined to be correct. For example, if the IRS determines the value to be only $5,000 and you claimed a $12,000 value (240 percent more), you are hung for a penalty. There are two ways to determine the penalty depending on the type of property involved:

1. Other Than Charitable Deduction Property

Ratio of Claimed Valuation to Correct Valuation	Penalty Percentage
150% to 200%	10%
Over 200% to 250%	20
Over 250%	30

NOTE

An overstatement of adjusted basis caused by overvaluation (for example, valuation of property in an estate) is treated like a valuation overstatement.

2. Charitable Deduction Property

Penalty is a 30 percent additional tax underpayment due to the valuation overstatement.

EXAMPLE

The IRS determines you owe an additional $2,000 in taxes after a downward adjustment of the property value claimed as a contribution deduction. The penalty is $600 (30 percent of $2,000).

DEFINITION

"Charitable deduction property" is any property contributed by an individual, closely held corporation or personal service corporation for which a charitable contribution has been claimed.

Valuation Understatement

The penalty applies if (Section 6660):

1. The understatement is made on a federal estate or gift tax return;
2. Because of the understatement, there is a tax underpayment of $1,000 or more; and
3. The value of the property claimed on the gift or estate tax return is 66-2/3 percent or less than the value finally determined.

NOTE
The penalty can be waived by the IRS if you can show a reasonable basis for the claimed value and that the claim was made in good faith.

The penalty, which is based on the amount of tax underpayment, is determined as follows:

Ratio of Claimed Valuation to Correct Valuation	Penalty Percentage
Over 50%, but not over 66-2/3%	10%
Over 40%, but less than 50%	20
Less than 40%	30

EXAMPLE
Joe's $42,000 valuation on a gift tax return ends up being $100,000 (42 percent of correct value) after an IRS audit. This causes an additional tax of $25,000. Joe's penalty is $5,000 (20 percent of $25,000).

HOW TO TEST YOUR VALUATION RESULT

Often, logic alone dictates that your valuation is too high or low. Then, the appraiser must take another look. Let's face it, it is difficult to explain unsupported logic or a gut feeling to an adversary on the other side of the table, the IRS or the courts.

But we are in luck: There is a practical way to test a high or low valuation. The liquidation value of a business is the floor value of any valuation. No matter what method or combination of methods causes the valuation to dip below liquidation value, the result can be disregarded. Your mission then becomes to determine liquidation value and that becomes fair market value.

NOTE
At best, liquidation value is an estimated figure. It is determined by estimating what would be the amount of cash in hand if every asset on the company's balance sheet was sold. For this purpose, cash can mean "cash and notes." All the liabilities of the company and the cost of liquidating each asset (appraiser fees, real estate fees, brokerage commissions, legal and accounting fees, etc.) then must be subtracted from the total cash received to determine the net liquidation value.

If net liquidation is the floor — the test for a low valuation — is there a way to test the ceiling — a high valuation? Yes. A crude but effective way to explain the method (sometimes called the "ceiling valuation test") is to repeat something a client told me after returning from a valuation seminar. He said that the seminar instructor, with tongue in cheek, said this about the buyer's viewpoint: "I don't care what the seller wants for the business. The selling price is not all that important. Just let me set the terms." And those terms will depend upon how much cash the buyer has in hand. The "terms" means how the balance of the price is to be paid: amount of payments, over what period of time, interest rate, etc. The point is that if the buyer can meet the terms, i.e., make the payments out of the cash flow of the purchased business, the price isn't too high.

On the other hand, if the payments cannot be made out of the cash flow of the business being bought, the price is too high, or the terms forcing the high payments are too steep, or both. From our viewpoint, when valuing a restaurant, one way to look at the transactions is through the eyes of a willing buyer. It is a three-step process:

1. Set down the most likely price and terms.
    a. Price
    b. Terms
        i. Amount down;
        ii. Number of months or years to pay; and
        iii. Rate of interest.
2. Make a cash flow projection considering the after-tax profit of the restaurant being bought.
3. Vary the price, terms and cash flow projections. Usually, at least three variations are required — best, most likely and worst scenario.

Each projection should be carried out for as many years as is necessary to show that the restaurant can (or cannot) meet the required payments and pay off the balance due.

What Is the Highest Price You Should Pay (or Sell For)?

The ceiling valuation amount in the practical sense is the highest amount that will enable the purchased restaurant to pay for itself over a reasonable period of time out of its available cash flow. One caveat: Approximately 20 percent to 40 percent of the available cash flow should be kept as a reserve for unforeseen contingencies. This is particularly true when the buyer is purchasing a new restaurant that will be his one and only business. If the buyer has an existing business that can subsidize any short-fall in the cash flow of the purchased restaurant, the contingency reserve can be narrowed and, in some cases, even eliminated.

OTHER FACTORS THAT CAN AFFECT PRICE (VALUATION)

Suppose that the fair market value has been determined using the appropriate methods as detailed in this book. Here are some factors that can raise or lower the price in an actual negotiation between a real buyer and a real seller:

1. Leverage vs. Cash

An all-cash transaction almost always produces a lower price. Installment sales should yield a higher price: The longer the term, assuming a market rate of interest, the higher the price is likely to be. Another general rule to keep in mind is that the more leveraged the transaction, the higher the purchase price.

2. Security to Seller

Often the seller does not want all cash. Why? All cash can cause a higher tax bill. So, the seller wants two things: first, to string the payments out for a designated period of time and, second, the maximum security possible to collateralize the note received for the non-cash balance. The collateral might include the buyer's personal signature, the stock or assets being purchased or other assets of the buyer. As a rule, the greater the security, the lower the purchase price (value of the business). Put another way, the greater the amount of cash or security at the time of closing, the greater the discount on the valuation of the business.

3. Form of Sale

When the business is appraised for the purposes of sale, the form of the sale impacts on the ultimate price. There are two reasons: the tax effect and the assump-tion of liabilities. There are two basic forms (methods) of selling a corporate business:

(1) sell the stock (assume 100 percent) or (2) sell the assets. Which method is the best way to buy a particular business for tax reasons is an important and complex subject and must be explored in depth with the help of a tax expert.

In general, a sale of stock is preferred by the seller because (1) he simply pays one tax on his profit, (2) all corporate liabilities are assumed by the buyer as the new owner of the corporation and (3) he does not get taxed at the corporate level for depreciation recapture (ordinary income) when the corporation sells the assets.

On the other hand, the buyer usually wants to buy only the assets because (1) he does not have to worry about corporate liabilities — known or unknown — and (2) he gets a new depreciation basis for the assets he purchases. Now then, add these two facts together when there is an asset purchase: (1) The seller gets stung for more taxes (reducing his after-tax profit), and (2) the buyer can reduce his tax bill because of a larger depreciation deduction, improving his after-tax cash flow. Both of these facts tend to increase the value of the assets being purchased.

4. Amount of Interest

A rate of interest greater than the current market value on the unpaid purchase price balance should lower the purchase price. Vice versa is the result for a lower-than-market rate of interest. In general, if the interest rate charged is less than a current market rate, the tax law imputes a market rate of interest for tax purposes. This raises the interest and lowers the purchase price as far as the IRS is concerned.

5. The "How-Much-Can-I-Pay" Formula

The highest price any buyer should pay for a business should be controlled by the "how-much-can-I-pay" formula. Here is the formula: a price at which the company has the ability to pay for itself, with a reasonable cushion for a margin of error, over a reasonable length of time. The formula can be reduced to numbers taking the following steps:

1. After the initial cash payment at closing, determine the time frame over which payments should be made (usually 5 to 10 years) to pay off the balance due.
2. Project the net available cash for the time frame selected. Make sure to add back depreciation to the after-tax profit and deduct required capital expenditures. If the cash flow will not retire the debt, the price paid is too high or the terms must be renegotiated. Terms include every factor that affects your ability to make payments: when payments start, how much each payment will be (including interest), for how long payments are to be made, what are your rights if a payment is late, etc.
3. Allow 60 percent to 80 percent of the net available cash for debt retirement; the balance (20 percent to 40 percent) should be considered a reserve to handle the cash needed for the unexpected.

And in Conclusion —

Now you are ready to go forth and conquer the valuation world. And as I have been telling my clients for years, "If you have any questions, call me."

CHAPTER IX

SAMPLE VALUATION

The valuation contained in this chapter was prepared by our office. All names, locations and some other data were changed to prevent identification of the client. The sample contains excerpts of the valuation text but very little of the supporting financial data. You or your professionals are welcome to use any of the material word for word.

PURPOSE OF VALUATION

The purpose of this valuation is to determine the fair market value of the 50 percent interest in two classes of common stock of Restaurant, Inc., owned by Jason Fooder at the date of his death, April 15, 1988. The results of the valuation are to be used to determine the estate tax value under Section 2031 of the Internal Revenue Code.

BRIEF DESCRIPTION OF BUSINESS

Restaurant, Inc., was founded in the late 1920s by the father of the present owners. It began with a single family restaurant and expanded to acquiring and building restaurants. The company operates a chain of restaurants in its home state.

The company has made numerous real estate investments for restaurant and non-restaurant use. It still owns property not being used in restaurant operations. The deceased was co-owner with his brother, Cliff Fooder, until his death.

As of April 15, 1988, Restaurant, Inc.'s capital structure consisted of the following:

Class	Authorized Shares	Outstanding Shares
Class A – Voting Common Stock	25,000	18,538
Class B – Non-voting Common Stock	25,000	18,538
Non-voting Preferred Stock	3,000	2,596

On April 15, 1988, Jason Fooder owned 9,269 shares of Class A Voting Common Stock and 9,269 shares of Class B Non-voting Common Stock. His brother owns the remaining shares of the common stock.

ANALYSIS OF FINANCIAL STATEMENTS

The following sources of information were used and relied upon for the valuation:
1. Audited financial statements of Restaurant, Inc., for the periods ended December 31, 1983, through December 31, 1987.
2. Unaudited and unadjusted financial statements for the four-month period ended April 30, 1988.
3. Standard and Poor's *Industry Surveys.*
4. *Industrial Norms and Key Business Ratios, 1986-1987*, Dun and Bradstreet.
5. *Almanac of Business and Industrial Financial Ratios.*
6. Information furnished by management of the company.
7. Other sources as cited in the body of this report.
Financial and statistical information from the above sources is deemed to be reliable. However, we make no representation as to our sources' accuracy or completeness and have accepted their information without further verification.

(Various financial data followed, which is not shown.)

In summary, the comparative financial analysis indicates the following:
- Limited sales growth has occurred over the past few years.
- The company has experienced poor profitability over the past few years. However, the poor profitability may be partially attributable to its relatively large amount of depreciation allowance from its high level of fixed asset investment in comparison to the industry norm.

- There are potential profits in the future because the company's food costs have improved modestly since 1984 in spite of competitive pressures.
- Even with a substantial investment in fixed assets, the company's ability to meet its current liabilities in 1987 remains adequate, as its current ratio is within the norm of the lower industry quartile. Also, its stockholders' equity to total assets is close to that of the industry norm.
- Its asset composition deviates greatly from the industry norm, as its fixed asset investment is nearly twice as large as the industry norm in 1987. Economic good will might not be present due to the company's recent poor operating results. Nonetheless, its large investment in carefully selected real estate indicates a going business concern with a value over and above the book value reflected on the books of the business.

SPECIFIC VALUATION METHODS

We have considered four basic approaches toward valuing the 50 percent common stock ownership interest of Restaurant, Inc., as follows:
1. Net book value approach;
2. Adjusted book value approach;
3. Capitalized earnings approach; and
4. Market comparison approach.

Selection of Valuation Techniques

We have considered all of the foregoing approaches and have selected the appropriate method to correspond to the specific circumstances of Restaurant, Inc., as of the valuation date. For various reasons discussed later, the value of Restaurant, Inc., has been determined on a going concern basis, with primary reliance on the adjusted net asset approach. Each method and the underlying philosophies are described in the following pages and considered in relation to the circumstances of the company.

Net Book Value Approach

The net book value approach (or net equity method) implies that a company is worth its accumulated retained earnings or deficit plus its original capitalization. There have been litigated cases where either the Internal Revenue Service or the taxpayer contended that the fair market value of stock approximated its book value. The courts in all such cases generally rejected the contention that book value approximated the fair market value of capital stock.

The primary reason the net book value approach is not relied upon as a good method of ascertaining the fair market value of Restaurant, Inc., is the substantial real estate owned by the company. The real estate has appreciated substantially, and its fair market value is substantially higher than its original cost less accumulated depreciation.

Adjusted Book Value Approach

One of the key inherent weaknesses of the net book value method, namely, that historical cost-based asset value may bear very little relationship to market value, is overcome in the adjusted net book value approach.

The adjusted book value method requires that all assets be evaluated to determine their true economic value. Fixed assets are appraised at a figure approximating their market value as opposed to depreciated cost.

This approach is used in cases (e.g., in bankruptcy proceedings) where the assets are actually to be liquidated following their acquisition. This method also is appropriate in those entities where economic goodwill is not present but whose assets are collectively employed in such a way as to produce a going concern and contain a value over and above what is recorded on the books of the business. This approach is applicable to companies having erratic or depressed earnings that are inadequate to provide a fair return on the value of the net tangible assets employed. In theory, the value of all assets, less all outstanding liabilities, provides an indication of the fair market value of ownership equity.

In Rev. Rul. 59-60, the IRS also indicates that the net asset value can be the primary consideration for valuing closely held investment or real estate holding companies.

Because of the depressed earnings of Restaurant, Inc., from 1985 through 1987, coupled with its relatively large real estate holdings, we believe that the adjusted net book value approach should be relied upon for determining the fair market value of the company.

Capitalized Earnings Approach

Conceptually, the capitalized earnings approach determines the fair market value of an ongoing business enterprise based on its earnings capacity. This approach is based on the theory that an investment (i.e., net tangible assets) will yield a return sufficient to recover its initial cost and to justly compensate the investor for the inherent risks of ownership. This approach is often used to arrive at a value for a company that reflects the company's goodwill due to its earnings in excess of the industry norm.

What constitutes a reasonable return on net tangible assets can best be answered by referring to Rev. Rul. 68-609, which states:

"The percentage of return on the average annual value of tangible assets used should be the percentage prevailing in the industry involved at the date of valuation."

From 1985 through 1987, Restaurant, Inc., experienced losses. Thus, its past losses tend to indicate that the company does not have goodwill (i.e., excess earnings) that can be quantified currently. Although future earnings are to be used for earnings capitalization, past earnings are usually the guide for determining future earnings. In this regard, Rev. Rul. 59-60 states, "Prior earnings records usually are the most reliable guide as to the future expectancy." In view of past losses, the company's future earnings are uncertain. Accordingly, we believe that the capitalized earnings approach should not be relied upon to value the company because the capitalization of losses would produce an unrealistic negative value.

Market Comparison Approach

The market comparison approach involves selecting public companies that are in the same or similar businesses and using their price earnings multiples as a guide in determining the value of the subject company. Price-earnings multiples established in active trading represent the market's fair rates of return on the investment. They are considered as being reliable indicators of the fair capitalization rates for the subject company, as appropriately adjusted for the risk factors associated with the subject company.

Finding price-earnings multiples of comparable publicly traded companies is a more difficult task than might be imagined. Often, finding even one listed company comparable to a closely held company is no easy task. In fact, such a comparable company might not exist. Moreover, Restaurant, Inc., has been experiencing losses over the past years. Applying price-earnings multiples to Restaurant, Inc., would create a negative value to the company as a whole. Accordingly, using price-earnings multiples of publicly traded companies would not be meaningful.

Computations of Adjusted Net Asset

As indicated previously, we believe that the adjusted net asset approach should be relied upon in determining the value of Restaurant, Inc. This approach involves adjusting the company's net assets from a book value basis to an approximation of market value. We made the following adjustments to the assets:

1. Convert investments and securities to approximate market value from cost. Some of the adjustments, for investments in privately held companies, are based on company management's estimations.

2. Mark up fixed assets to an approximation of market value. The adjustments are based on an appraisal of these assets.

3. Incorporate the approximate after-tax loss during the period from January 1, 1988, through April 30, 1988. This adjustment is a rough approximation based on unaudited financial statements provided by company management. Such an adjustment is necessary to account for the change in net assets from the audited financial statements as of December 31, 1987, through April 30, 1988.

4. Proceeds received by the corporation as the beneficiary of Jason Fooder's life insurance policy.

Valuation of Common Stock Interest

Since our purpose is to value the common stock, it is necessary to determine how much of the $3,982,969 adjusted net asset value is allocable to the common stock interest.

As of April 15, 1986, the company had 2,596 shares of outstanding non-voting preferred stock. The preferred stock is callable at $100 par value, with a 5 percent cumulative dividend rate.

It is not our objective here to value the preferred stock. Our goal is to determine the portion of the adjusted net asset value that is allocable to the common stock interest. A prudent investor planning to purchase only the common stock would allocate the adjusted net asset value to the preferred stock at the par value, as the preferred stock is callable at par and has a liquidation preference at par. A preferred stock having a market value less than its par value does not necessarily mean that the value attrition would increase the portion of the adjusted net asset value allocable to the common stock. Accordingly, the adjusted net asset value allocable to the common stock should be determined by accounting for the preferred stock at its par value, as follows:

Adjusted net asset value	$3,982,969
Less amount allocated to preferred stock at $100 par value per share	($259,600)
Adjusted net asset value allocable to the two classes of common stock	$3,723,369
Shares of common stock outstanding	37,076
Adjusted net asset value per share of common stock	$100.43

DISCOUNT FOR GENERAL LACK OF MARKETABILITY AND NON-CONTROLLING INTEREST

The adjusted net asset value figure of $3,723,369 allocable to common stock is a value based on intrinsic factors (i.e., the aggregate values of the underlying assets). Since Restaurant, Inc., is a closely held business, a discount for general lack of marketability is appropriate. The lack of marketability discount concept recognizes the fact that closely held stock interests are less attractive and have fewer potential purchasers than similar publicly traded stock.

The principle of a discount for lack of marketability has been stated as follows:

"It seems clear...that an unlisted closely held stock of a corporation..., in which trading is infrequent and which therefore lacks marketability, is less attractive than a similar stock which is listed on an exchange and has ready access to the investing public" (*Central Trust Co.*, 305 F2d 393 (CtCl 1962)).

If the owners of closely held stocks should try to list a block of such securities on a stock exchange for sale to the public, they would probably have to make the offerings through underwriters. There would be costs for registering non-publicly traded stocks with the Securities and Exchange Commission (SEC), involving (among other fees) the expense of preparing a prospectus. In addition, the underwriters themselves would receive commissions. The actual costs of such an offering can range from 10 percent to 25 percent of the selling price to the public.

A study on marketability discounts for closely held business interests was done by J. Michael Maher ("Discounts for Lack of Marketability for Closely Held Business Interests," *Taxes* (September 1986), pp. 562-71). The study involves a comparison of the price paid for restricted stocks with the market prices of their unrestricted counterparts. The study shows that "the mean discount for lack of marketability for the years 1969-73 amounted to 35.43 percent." Maher then makes an interesting second computation, eliminating the top 10 percent and the bottom 10 percent of purchases to remove especially high- and low-risk situations; the result was almost identical with a mean discount of 34.73 percent.

Maher concludes:

"The result I have reached is that most appraisers underestimate the proper discount for lack of marketability. The results seem to indicate that this discount should be about 35 percent. Perhaps this makes sense because by committing funds to restricted common stock, the willing buyer (a) would be denied the opportunity to take advantage of other investments and (b) would continue to have his investment at the risk of the business until the shares could be offered to the public or another buyer is found.

"The 35 percent discount would not contain elements of a discount for a minority interest because it is measured against the current fair market value of securities actively traded (other minority interests). Consequently, appraisers should also consider a discount for a minority interest in those closely held corporations where a discount is applicable."

Recent cases in valuation provided substantial discounts for non-marketability and other inhibiting factors. In *Estate of Arthur F. Little, Jr.* (TCM 1982-26, CCH Dec. 38729(M)), the Tax Court allowed a total discount of 60 percent for shares of restricted stock of a publicly held company. The court allowed a 35 percent discount for sales restrictions, a 15 percent discount for an irrevocable two-year voting proxy agreement and a 10 percent discount for shares that were held in escrow.

In *William T. Piper, Sr. Est.* (72 TC No. 88, CCH Dec. 36,315), the court allowed a total discount of 64 percent for stock of a corporation that owned publicly traded securities and rental property. The court allowed a discount of 35 percent for lack of marketability, 17 percent for relatively unattractive investment portfolios and another 12 percent for possible stock registration costs.

In *Estate of Mark S. Gallo* (TCM 1985-363, CCH Dec. 42241(m)), the Tax Court allowed a discount of 36 percent for general lack of marketability.

Of particular interest is the **Estate of Ernest E. Kirkpatrick** (CCH Dec. 33,524(M), 34 TCM 1490, 1975). In this case, the court found per-share value without mentioning discount. However, expert witnesses for both the IRS and the taxpayer used a 50 percent discount to reflect the stock's lack of marketability and minority interest.

In addition to the general lack of marketability as discussed above, the 50 percent interest in common stock owned by Jason Fooder does not represent a controlling interest in the company. An acquisition of such interest does not afford a potential purchaser the power to fully influence management and day-to-day business operations. An acquisition of a 50 percent interest may afford a greater discount than a mere discount for the general lack of marketability. Put another way, the value of a non-controlling interest (50 percent or less) is lower than the per-share value of an interest in the same company that would have control (more than 50 percent).

The extent to which any restriction on marketability and inhibiting factors reduces the value of a specific stock is determined based on facts and circumstances. In view of the depressed earnings of Restaurant, Inc., over the recent past years, the non-controlling block of stock and the general lack of marketability factors, a 30 percent discount is appropriate for the valuation of the 50 percent voting common stock owned by Jason Fooder. An additional 10 percent discount is appropriate for the valuation of the other 50 percent non-voting common stock owned by Jason Fooder. This additional 10 percent discount accounts for the non-voting privileges of the stock. As held in **Estate of Arthur F. Little, Jr.**, the Tax Court allows a 15 percent discount for an irrevocable two-year voting proxy agreement.

	Class A Voting	Class B Non-voting
Adjusted net asset value per share	$100.43	$100.43
Less		
Discount for general lack of marketability, non-controlling interest and depressed earnings – 30%	(30.13)	(30.13)
Discount for non-voting privilege –10%		(10.04)
Adjusted net asset value per share after discount	$ 70.30	$ 60.26

CONCLUSION

Based on the information and analyses summarized in this report, it is our opinion that, as of April 15, 1988, the fair market value of each of the two classes of common stock held by Jason Fooder is as follows:

	Common Stock		
	Class A Voting	Class B Non-voting	Total
Value per share	$70.30	$60.26	
Number of shares held	9,269	9,269	
Total value	$651,611	$558,550	$1,210,161

1952-2
22-10